# Vegetarianism
## in the political debate

EZEQUIEL MARTÍN ARRIETA

ARRIETA, EZEQUIEL MARTÍN
Vegetarianism in the political debate
1era Edición Córdoba: el autor
13,97x21,59 – 266 pp.

ISBN-13: 978-1501022067
ISBN-10: 1501022067

Translation: Graglia, María Agustina; Grobisa, Nicolás;
Lofiego, Daniela; Madonna, Fátima; Palacín, Federico.

Proofreading: Graglia, María Agustina; Lofiego,
Daniela; Madonna, Fátima.

Cover design: Madonna, Fátima

Diagramation and design: Villarroel Bertoldi, Joel
Alejandro.

# Acknowledgements

To all those people who dedicate their lives to build a better world.

To all of those people who fight each day for knowledge to be recognized as heritage of humanity.

To the people who are part of movements that are becoming stronger, like the free software movement, free culture, free science and free education.

To all those people who recognize the importance of keeping a free Internet and fight for that.

To all of you, my greatest thanks. You are the unrecognized heroes of this generation.

# Author's preface

*Translation: María Agustina Graglia*

It is time to face the overwhelming evidence of how unsustainable an inefficient the current food system is when based on animal source foods. We urgently need society to understand the economic, environmental and political fragility we are in, and at the same time we need to make approaches towards new strategies that will allow us to adapt to the current (and future) reality.

Food consumption patterns have enormously contributed to this situation, since there have been changes in the dietary composition developing exponentially since the 60s and worldwide. These changes happened because of an increase in the consumption of animal source foods (meat, dairy and eggs). Even though I consider all exploitation of sentient beings to be an unnecessary act (except for biomedical experimentation for which I take a neutral stance), the ethical motivations that led me to write this book are those concerning human beings. The trend of consumption of animal source foods threatens the attempts for sustainability.

The growing consumption of livestock products negatively affects nations' food safety, directly by providing animals with great amounts of food that could be consumed by humans, and indirectly by affecting the environment (on which we depend to produce food) in many ways, such as deforestation, decreased water availability because of its use, watersheds pollution and degradation, biodiversity loss, soil degradation, contributing to global warming and climate change by increasing greenhouse gases, and contributing to desertification and environmental pollution by improperly using agrochemicals.

We are talking about a situation that concerns us all, an issue that should be approached with utmost seriousness. I invite you to dive into this book where I will try to expand, through the presentation of arguments based on scientific evidence and verifiable data, the reasons why vegetarianism should be in the political debate.

I invite you not only to read it, but also to do it from a skeptical attitude. Skepticism is often subject of criticism, but in this line of thought it is traditionally an honorable activity, as demonstrated by the etiology of the term (which is of Greek origin and means "reflection"). This is a worthwhile clarification because, although we generally consider ourselves to be rational beings, neurobiology research has demonstrated that our brain is not "programed" to be rational, therefore being rational takes a lot of work. We are clearly emotional beings and we are driven by emotions, which proves why so many people have behave irrationally and are capable of the most heinous horrors. Unless we use reason rigorously to discover and recognize the objectivity of nature and stick to the logical consequences of our findings in order to engage in efficient actions, we will fall into the hands of the feared forces of irrationality, of romanticism and of the apparent inevitability of mass behavior.

Reason is not only a very important part of our essence, it is also our potential savior from the fierce and precipitated mass action that the emotional governance seems to carry along with. Skepticism is the active agent of reason, it faces organized irrationality and it is therefore one of the keys to civic and social decency.

We must also remind ourselves that science progresses as evidence-gathering methods improve, either by a better understanding of natural phenomena or by a greater development of technologies and techniques that help increase the available knowledge on different subjects.

Thus, people should begin to realize that critical thinking is essential for us to tackle problems that lash us. It is not a matter of opinions and beliefs, it is a matter of facts. And facts should at least have a higher level of hierarchy than cultural conceptions when it comes to the environment and health.

On the other hand, authorities must urgently assume their responsibilities and guide the population towards adopting a sustainable diet. Likewise, it is necessary to develop policies that encourage the consumption of the foods involved in that diet, and to improve their production from a sustainability point of view.

Finally, I want to express with all due respect to the people who are vegetarians, that the above-described makes it imperative to take this debate beyond the personal sphere. We must put aside mysticism, religion and New Age doctrines that have so much impregnated vegetarianism throughout the years, especially during the last decade. It is necessary for us to educate ourselves and to know the evidence that supports this idea, if we want this diet to be taken into account in the political debate.

*Ezequiel Martín Arrieta.*

# I     *Index*

# Introduction

*Translation: Nicolás Grobisa*

A thorough analysis of the impact produced by livestock on health and environment gives us some notion of the great responsibility animal production has in terms of earth and water degradation, biodiversity, climate change, and exponential growth of the so-called "modern diseases" derived from animal product consumption.

The livestock sector is one of the top two or three sectors with the most serious repercussions on the environment, at every scale from local to global [Stenfield *et al*, 2006]. Its impact is so significant that it demands immediate attention, taking into account that remarkable benefits could be obtained at a reasonable cost.

Agriculture is going to face multiple challenges during the 21st century, such as producing more food for a continuously growing population, increasing raw material production for the potential biofuels market, applying more efficient and sustainable methods of production, and adapting itself to new challenges yielded by climate change and environmental degradation. Inevitably, there is an urgent need to take measures on the current food production model and the adopted diets. A rational walkout from meat production and consumption may result in huge benefits for the environment and human health.

But before reviewing data, it is necessary to clarify the meaning of the word *vegetarianism* in the context of this book. The Vegetarian Society defines a vegetarian as *"someone who lives on a diet of grains, pulses, nuts, seeds, vegetables and fruits with, or without, the use of dairy products and eggs"* [Vegetarian Society]. According to the National Institutes of Health of the United States, vegetarian diets can be classified as [NIH, 2014]:

- Strict vegetarian (or vegan): plant foods exclusively.
- Lacto vegetarian: plant foods with the addition of dairy products.
- Lacto-ovo vegetarian: plant foods with the addition of both dairy and eggs.

It is also necessary to differentiate between the terms *veganism* and *vegetarianism*, due to recurrent confusion between them. According to a 1979 Memorandum of Association of the Vegan Society, veganism denotes a *"philosophy and way of living which seeks to exclude — as far as is possible and practical — all forms of exploitation of, and cruelty to, animals for food, clothing or any other purpose; and by extension, promotes the development and use of animal-free alternatives for the benefit of humans, animals and the environment"* [Vegan Society]. This leads us to understand that veganism is not a diet, but an ethical behavior based on the rejection of any kind of exploitation of other sentient beings, considered as useful properties, merchandise, or mere consumption products. However, since vegans live on a strict vegetarian diet, there is a tendency to confuse both the terms vegan and vegetarian (or veganism and vegetarianism).

So, from now on, whenever the word *vegetarianism* is used in this book, it will be in reference to the practice of following any of the forementioned vegetarian diets, which includes the strict vegetarian diet adopted by vegans.

Once these concepts are clear, one can wonder: **are meat production and consumption sustainable?** Apparently not, and that is what I will try to explain and uphold throughout this book.

Food consumption and production tendencies are some of the main causes of pressure on the environment. In order to achieve a sustainable development, it is imperative that fundamental changes happen in the way food is produced, processed, transported, and consumed.

In ecology, the term *sustainability* refers to the capacity of biological systems to endure and remain productive. However, it also refers to the equilibrium between a species and the consumption of resources in order to meet the needs of the present without compromising the future [Magee *et al*, 2013].

*Sustainable food consumption and production* is a holistic

concept. Therefore, it demands the consideration of all aspects of a product: its production, its consumption, its consumers' lifestyles and their adopted diets, loss management, waste, recycling, sustainability standards, and methods and processes for reducing the negative effects on the environment as much as possible.

Food and agricultural systems are developed within a finite base of resources which, very frequently, tend to be rather limited. Thus, it is necessary for these sectors to use natural resources sensibly in order to preserve the ecosystem. Growth of these systems must be inclusive and need to focus on goals that go beyond mere production and economic growth.

In 2010, in the scientific symposium named "Biodiversity and Sustainable Diets – United Against Hunger", FAO (Food and Agriculture Organization of the United Nations) issued a report where the term *sustainable diets* was coined for the first time, defined as *"diets with low environmental impacts which contribute to food and nutrition security and to healthy life for present and future generations"* [FAO, 2010]. It also expressed that *"sustainable diets are protective and respectful of biodiversity and ecosystems, culturally acceptable, accessible, economically fair and affordable; nutritionally adequate, safe and healthy; while optimizing natural and human resources"* [FAO, 2010]. In August of 2012, FAO published a book entitled "Sustainable Diets and Biodiversity" [FAO & Biodiversity International, 2012] where there is a stress on the need to act immediately and promote sustainable diets in order to improve the overall health for humans and the planet. Barbara

Burlingame, PhD, -Senior Officer and Leader of the Nutrition Requirements and Assessment Group for the FAO- says in the book preface: *"Regardless of the many successes of agriculture during the last three decades, it is clear that food systems, and diets, are not sustainable"*.

Despite the fact that it has not been defined what a sustainable diet is and what should be based on, most experts agree that it should be poor in animal source foods and rich in vegetables, fruits and whole grains. But, in order to conclude that animal source food consumption is not sustainable, we need to approach evidence from the economical, environmental and sanitarian scopes.

# Chapter 2

## Economy and Food Security

*Translation: Daniela Lofiego*

### 2.1 Distorted Values

It may be necessary to address a little bit of Economy to justify how and why meat consumption is inefficient. Many associate Economy to numbers, equations, and financial crisis, causing contempt towards this simple, obvious, and important subject.

According to the Royal Academy of the Spanish Language (RAE), economy is the *"science that studies the most efficient methods to satisfy material human needs through the use of scarce goods"* [RAE].

But, how does the current already obsolete socio-economic system influence this science?

The current socio-economic system (in which free market is the main model), has distorted the human beings' needs-hierarchy, placing first those related to grandiosity and superficiality above those which are vital, like clean water, pure air, nutritive food, shelter and relevant education. The system of values instilled by this society based on competition and individualism has nothing to do with integrity, justice, collaboration, respect and honesty [Hurt, 2012].

This is why administering scarce resources in an efficient manner is not a matter of importance for people, whether they are authorities, entrepreneurs, or the rest of the population. Due to this intrinsic system failure, a great number of projects which were meant to abolish hunger, malnutrition, poverty or social inequality have resulted null through the last 40 years, as we shall see next.

## 2.2 War against hunger?

In 1974, governments attending The World Food Conference proclaimed that *"every man, woman and child have the inalienable right to be free from hunger and malnutrition in order to develop their physical and mental faculties"* [FAO, 1999]. The Conference set as its goal the eradication of hunger, food insecurity, and malnutrition within a decade. At that moment it was estimated that there were about 460 million people suffering from hunger, around 40% of which were children and the great majority were living in third world countries [Abel-Smith & Leiserson, 1978]. Nevertheless, some considered these numbers had to be greater due to the unreliable statistics at that moment [Viera-Gallo, 1977].

In the World Food Summit of 1996 representatives from 185 countries and the European Union committed to fight and eradicate hunger. As a first decisive step they set as target to halve the number of people suffering from hunger by the year 2015. Authorities looked optimistic by that time. Some statements by the members of the event are well known, for example, Prof. Romano Prodi, PhD, (Chairman of the event) said *"The Rome Declaration calls upon us to reduce by half the number of chronically undernourished people on the Earth by the year 2015..... If each of us gives his or her best I believe that we can meet and even exceed the target we have set for ourselves."* On the other hand, Jaques Diouf, PhD, (Director General of FAO) claimed that: *"We have the possibility to do it. We have the knowledge. We have the resources. And with the Rome Declaration and the Plan of Action, we have shown that we have the will"* [FAO, 1999].

In the year 2000, the Millennium Declaration was passed by 189 countries and signed by 147 presidents in the United Nations Millennium Summit, held in September of 2000 [UNDP, 2014]. The Millennium Development Goals (MDGs), are eight ambitious goals that have to be met by the year 2015; they are based on the activities and proposals included in the Millennium Declaration, which reads *"To halve, by the year 2015, the percentage of inhabitants whose daily income are less than a dollar and people suffering from hunger; likewise, by that date, halve the percentage of people who have no access or cannot afford clean water"* [UN, 2000].

In the year 2009 hunger reached its upper limit. FAO estimated that 1.02 billion people are undernourished due to the world economic recession, almost a sixth of the world

27

population [FAO, 2009a]. Four years later, the World Food Programme, confirmed that 868 million people were still suffering from hunger, this constituted then a higher health issue compared to HIV, malaria and tuberculosis put together [WFP, 2014]. Besides, the great majority of people with hunger, 98%, live in developing countries, where almost 15% of the population is undernourished [FAO, 2012a].

Undernourishment contributes to the death of 2.6 million children under the age of 5 every year, a third of the global total [UNICEF, 2011]. One out of four kids has delayed growth [UNICEF, 2012] and within these, 80% are distributed in only 20 countries [Bryce *et al*, 2008].

These alarming statistics take place in spite of the dramatic increase in food production since the decade of the 60s (between 70% and 280% depending on the source) [Rudela *et al*, 2009; Royal Society, 2009], and despite the number of congresses, summits, conferences, reunions and protests held to stop world hunger.

Nevertheless, some signs have been given in relation to the need of a change of approach, as mentioned in the report "The State of Food Insecurity in the World 2012" [FAO, 2012a]: economic growth is not sufficient to accelerate reduction of hunger and malnutrition. This led the United Nations Environment Programme (UNEP) to write a report called: "Avoiding Famines in the Future: Strengthening the Ecological Basis of Food Security through Sustainable Food Systems" to be shown before the presidents at Rio+20. It emphasises the weakening of the ecological basis of the current food system, already unsustainable over time due to the great environmental impacts it produces, and the threat to the world's food security [UNEP, 2012].

## 2.3 Food Administration

In a system that works through profit, without taking into account social or environmental consequences, it is not hard to recognize why a meat (and meat derived products) based diet is encouraged. It is the clearest example of higher inefficiency in resource management because its production involves a great waste of water, soil and energy.

The established farming model is unsustainable. In the industrious meat production, cereals that could be used to feed people are used to feed the livestock. Something completely unacceptable if we have in mind, as aforementioned, that the number of people suffering from hunger in the world is 868 millions, according to the latest estimations [WFP, 2014]. Despite of this, food is not scarce.

We produce enough food to feed everyone. World agriculture produces 17% more calories per person today than it did 30 years ago, despite a 70% population increase. This quantity of food could provide everyone in the world with at least 2720 kilocalories (kcal) per person per day according to the most recent estimate that we could find [FAO, 2002]. This fact can be remarked with the fact that about 1.3 billion tons of food are thrown to the waste [FAO, 2011]. Nevertheless, not

29

many people have access to farming lands or have enough money incomes to buy them.

Although nowadays we are facing a problem of wrong food distribution, we cannot deny some obvious facts that are affecting us now, and will continue to affect us in years to come: population growth at an accelerated rate and environmental deterioration to a point of no return.

## 2.4 Livestock Production Systems

Current agricultural systems range from traditional small-scale subsistence agriculture (small farmers who depend on low cost and traditional knowledge), to conventional industrial large scale, agriculture that depends on great amounts of energy, fertilizers and other goods. Whether at small or large scale agriculture depends on the dominant sociocultural and biophysical settings.

In 1995, FAO classified the livestock systems in 11 groups according to the different systems of agricultural production, its relation to the soil and the agro-ecological area [FAO, 1995]. Three main systems can be identified:

• **Livestock systems based on pastures or Grazing**. Exclusively livestock production systems, frequently based on migratory grazing on seasonal pastures or highland pastures. This used to be located in the most marginal zones, not apt for agriculture, whether for low temperatures, scarce precipitations or topographic conditions. These produce around

12% of the milk and 9% of the world meat, and they occupy major land areas, also known as extensive livestock.

• **Mixed farming systems**. Production systems where animals eat grass, crop residues and fodde;, these can be found in ecosystems with better bioclimatic conditions and are responsible for 88% of milk production and 6% of meat production globally.

• **Intensive Industrial Production Systems (feed-lot)**. Systems in which animals are fed purchased fodder. These systems are dominant in areas with dense population with high income, in particular in the coastal regions in Southern Asia, Europe, and North America connected to sea ports for feed import. In contrast, there are areas with a great fodder offer, such as the Midwestern region in the United States and the inner regions in Brazil and Argentina where industrial systems, which use local cereal production surplus, have been developed. These systems are responsible for 45% of meat production and 61% of egg production globally.

Improvements in development and investigation in agriculture have introduced a great number of enhancements in agricultural practices. Nevertheless, many of these practices have great impacts on the environment, sometimes they strengthen and better the environmental conditions, and sometimes they weaken them. This is why, as demonstrated by the multiple agricultural state reports, ecosystems' environmental services and needed resources to support global agricultural production are being seriously undermined [World Bank, 2007; McIntyre *et al*, 2009; TGOS, 2011; The Development Fund, 2010; UNEP 2011].

## 2.5 Livestock and Food Production

Agriculture plays a very important role in human development since it provides with 90% of the world's caloric intake. Besides the provision of food, fibre and other biomaterials, the agricultural sector also employs a lot of people, especially in developing countries where it is considered a major source of income for the lower classes. Statistics show that around 2.6 billion people depend on some sort of agriculture to earn a living [IAASTD, 2009].

Nevertheless, somehow this is not being made the most of. The current food system is unsustainable and can be illustrated in a qualitative sense through an examination of the carbon footprint, the approximate amount of resources needed to produce food; and their environmental impacts. Through the use of this tool it has been estimated that by the year 2030 the resources of two planets Earth will be needed to feed, dress, and sustain world population in the current consumption average level [WWF/ZSL/GFN, 2010]. From what has been mentioned we will be able to analyze how we produce food.

According to the United Nations Convention to Combat Desertification, in the year 2009, 7 to 10 kg of cereals were needed to produce 1 kg of meat, this means that the annual grain consumption per capita in India (low meat intake) was about 180 kg while the grain consumption per capita in the United States (high meat intake) was around 725 kg: 2 kg of cereals per day [UNCCD, 2009]. Another report jointly published by the Wegener Centre and the Sustainable Europe Research Institute, indicated that around 0,25 and 1,82 kg of *"material supplies"* (needed resources for goods production) are needed to produce one kilogram of the majority of fruits and vegetables, 4,58 kg and 5,10 kg for the production of poultry and pork meat respectively, while this figures raise to 17,7 kg to produce 1 kg of beef, and 32,8 kg for dry, salt, and smoked meat [Friedl *et al*, 2007].

These values derive from the conversion of vegetal protein to animal protein, and 2 main costs are taken into account [Pimentel & Pimentel, 2003]:

1. Direct costs for food production for animals.
2. Indirect costs for offspring maintenance.

The use of fodder coming from the harvest of basic food as cereals and legumes has increased rapidly during the last decades as a response to a growth in fodder demand and the insufficient capacity traditional fodder has to supply the required nutrients both in quality and quantity. Among these, corn and oats are the most used with a percentage higher than 60% during the period 1961-2002 periods [Steinfield *et al*, 2006]. Corn is the main cereal in Brazil, China, Argentina and the United States where more than 70% is used as feed; while wheat and oats are the main ones in Canada and Europe [USDA, 2013]. Similar percentages in wheat can be found in

South Asia up to the beginnings of the 90s, when a gradual turn to corn happened [APAARI, 2012].

According to the "Food Outlook: Global Market Analysis 2014" report by FAO on May 2014, 35% of grains produced globally – among them 19% of wheat and 57% of total coarse grains (sorghum, millet, oats, rye and barley) production – were used to feed cattle [FAO, 2014].

In relation to soybeans we can say that, initially, oil production was a booster for the production of this leguminous plant, and today expansion obeys fundamentally to supply the fodder demand. Today, it represents two thirds of the global total production of protein food [Oil World, 2010], and its nutritious value cannot be beaten by any other vegetable protein source; it is the standard to which other protein sources are compared [Cromwell, 1999]. Although soybeans have been a dietary component for cattle and poultry in the United States since the mid 30s [Lewis & Southern, 2001], soybean production lifted off halfway through the 70s and then accelerated in the decade of the 90s due to an increase in demand from the developing countries. Expansion in aquaculture (fish production) and the banning of slaughterhouse sub products used as food has fuelled the demand of this high quality protein source [Steinfeld *et al*, 2006].

Only a small portion of harvested grains are given directly to animals (around 3%); what is actually used as fodder is soybean meal which constitutes the greater protein source for livestock. In the oil extraction process, soybean seeds produce between 18-19% oil and 73-74% soybean meal, the rest is waste. In 2012, soybean production of the 5 countries with the largest oilseed crops (United States, Brazil, Argentina, China and India), was about 212.3 million tonnes [FAO, 2012b]; more than 98% of world's soybean meal production is destined to fodder production to feed monogastric species, especially poultry, and to a lesser extent, swine [SoyTech, 2014].

Projections indicate a growth in livestock production and a resulting increase in fodder demand. According to the report "Food Outlook: Global Market Analysis 2014", monthly cereal production for year 2013 was 2.51 billion tons. [FAO, 2014], and FAO foresees that the demand of cereals for fodder will have an estimated increase of 1 billon tons for the period 1997/99 to 2030, an unprecedented growth rate. For the year 2050 more than 3 billon tons of grain will be produced [Alexandratos & Bruinsma, 2012].

Without a doubt, the relative change in stock production in regions that are now using intensive feeding systems based on grains made the grain/meat ratio lower. In the year 2012 cereal use for fodder was about 742 million tons; it is estimated that by the year 2050 it will be 1.113 billon tons [Alexandratos & Bruinsma, 2012].

## 2.6 Land for Livestock

Grains that are used to feed livestock must be cultivated in the soil, which requires the use of certain amount of space that will vary according to the demand: the higher consumption of stock derived products, the greater the grain demand to feed them; therefore, more space will be needed to grow their food (grain and pastures).

There are many factors that affect the amount of food livestock can consume, these include physiological factors (weight, breastfeeding period), environmental (temperature, humidity), dietary (type of food, fodder quality) and management (feed-lot, outdoors breeding). In average, an animal consumes between 1,6% and 3% of its weight in dry food per day; this is, besides the water contents, an average of 2% [Ag-Info Centre, 2013; Rasby, 2013]. For example, a cow weighing 544 kg (1200 pounds) will eat a total of 10,88 kg of dry food if we count the average intake of 2%, which sums a total of 3971,2 kg in dry food per year. In the case of milk cows, intake is greater, reaching 25 kg of dry food per day [Gómez, 2008].

To produce this amount of food you need quite a lot of space. This varies according to different factors such as rain regimes, type of seed, fertilizer usage, soil fertility, type of sowing, technology used in the process, weather adversities, etc. Argentina's estimates are the following:

- Corn: 7,4 tons/hectare [INTA, 2012].
- Wheat: 4,3 tons/hectare [INTA, 2013].
- Oats: 4,5 tons/hectare [INTA, 2011].
- Sorghum: 6,8 tons/hectare [Cicchino *et al*, 2012].
- Soybean: 2 tons/hectare [INTA, 2009].

Now we will see how much food humans consume to make an appreciation of the space used to cultivate grains for livestock feed. According to the Recommended Daily Intake (RDI) by the Institute of Medicine of the USA [Institute of Medicine, 2002], an average adult person need around 2200 kcal/day (kilocalories per day); these come from the macronutrients carbohydrates (45-60%), proteins (10-35%) and fat (20-35%). The energetic density of proteins is 4,1 kcal/grams, of carbohydrates is 4,2 kcal/grams and of fat is 9,5 kcal/grams [Sadava & Orians, 2000]. Supposing a person has a diet of 2200 kcal/day composed of 50% carbohydrates, 30% proteins and 20% fat, we can make some estimates. This person consumes a total amount of:

• 1100 kcal/day carbohydrates, that is equal to 261,9 grams/day.

• 660 kcal/day proteins that is equal to 160,9 grams/day.

• 440 kcal/day fat that is equal to 46,3 grams/day.

The aforementioned sums a total of 469,1 grams of macronutrients per day, which is 171.2 kg per year. We could say that many of us consume around 469,1 grams of food per day. Nevertheless, it is true that for this estimates we haven't taken into account the fibre nor the water contained which would add a lot to the food volume.

Values provided by the Economy Research Service from the U. S. Department of Agriculture, even if it is a region in the world that exceeds the recommended daily calorie intake, informs us that an average citizen of that country (of around 36 years old) consumes an average of 904.1 kg of food per year [CreditLoan, 2011; USDA, 2013]. Yes, almost a ton, which corresponded to an amount of 2,74 kg/day, which does not seem like a lot if we say it like that. With these numbers I want to compare what humans consume (904.1 kg/year) to what an average cow consumes (3971.2 kg/year) and connect it to the before mentioned: *"in the year 2013, 34% of cereals produced globally were used to feed cattle"*.

Then, **how many people could be fed on the food destined to livestock for meat production?**

We stated that livestock, depending on the farming system used, can be fed on pastures, fodder or both. In any case space is required to produce enough food. A report by the International Agricultural Research Institute mentions that 45% of the world's surface is used by livestock systems [Thornton *et al*, 2011]. Meanwhile, FAO indicates that livestock systems use 26% of the earth's surface, including permanent pastures (mainly) [Steinfeld *et al*, 2006] and Asner and colleagues estimate that grasslands account for about 2/3 of the total agricultural land in the world [Asner *et al*, 2004].

**What is the big deal with space if the Earth is so big?**

Well, theoretically there is a lot of land. The planet is big, more than we can imagine. But the demographic growth and the income increase, as well as the transformation of food choices are stimulating an accelerated increase in the demand of livestock products. Livestock systems have been, and are, an important factor in the agricultural growth globally. World's food economy is being increasingly driven more every day by the dietary changes and animal source products consumption patterns. Some have used the term *"Livestock Revolution"* to refer to this tendency [Delgado *et al*, 2001].

## 2.7 Increases in Animal Source Food Consumption

FAO's information indicates that livestock production grew rapidly as a result of the increasing demand in animal source products. Since 1960, world's meat production has more than tripled, milk has production almost duplicated, and egg production has increased in almost four times. This can be attributed, partly, to population increase and wealth increase in many countries [Speedy, 2003].

Global meat production in 1950 was 44 million tonnes, an average of 17,2 kg per person per year (kg/person/year); in 1970, it reached 100 million tonnes, and in 2002 it reached 242 million tonnes and an average of 39 kg/person/year [Nierenberg, 2003; EPI, 2013]. The tendency continued rising; in 2007, it reached 285.7 millions tonnes, and in 2013, 308.3 million tonnes [FAO, 2009b; FAO, 2013]. Estimated meat consumption per person for the year 2050 is around 49,4 kg/person/year, and if the population should continue growing (around 9 billion people for 2050), meat production will rise to 455 million tonnes, almost twice the current production [Alexandratos & Bruinsma, 2012].

But, let's not forget about dairy products, eggs and fish. These too are part of a diet based in animal source food, and its production is tied to almost all the same mechanisms as meat production. As I mentioned before, milk consumption also almost doubled in the last four decades, going from 470 million tonnes produced in 1981 to 780 million tonnes in 2013 [FAO 2013; FAO 2014]. Egg production went from 14.3 million tonnes in 1960 to 69.1 million tonnes in 2010; in the meantime, fish production went from 32.5 million tonnes in 1960 (some 8,9 kg/person/year) to 160 million tonnes in 2013 (19,1 kg/person/year in 2012) [EPI 2013; FAO 2014].

It's important to know these figures because the progressive increase in animal source food requires, too, an increase in the production of food destined to fodder. For the year 2050 cereal production will need to be increased in 940 million tonnes to reach the 3 billion tonnes needed to fill the fodder and human consumption requirements [FAO, 2012a].

## 2.8 Feeding a Growing Population

In a world that is more concerned in sustainable food production, ideally, livestock contribution to the dietary balance should at least be neutral. Nevertheless, this does not occur globally.

The most important contribution of livestock to the total availability of food is when it is produced in places where crops cannot grow so easily, like mountain marginal areas, arid zones, where it is possible to grow food that cannot be consumed directly by humans (pastures). In these situations, cattle is justified because it corresponds to an excellent source of nutrients that could hardly be made up for by other food; but when livestock is raised in intensive systems (as the feed-lot), it consumes the food that could be destined directly to humans, turning energy from carbohydrates and proteins in a less available quantity [FAO, 2011]. If we take into account that these systems provide 45% of meat and 61% of eggs, transformed nutrients' quantity is huge [FAO, 2009b]. To give you a notion, it is estimated that 77 million tonnes of vegetable source proteins are consumed annually by livestock to produce 58 million tonnes of animal source proteins [Steinfeld *et al*, 2006].

To provide the growing world population with enough food, both in quantity and quality, while protecting the natural ecosystems is one of our society's challenges. Last decades have witnessed an unprecedented human population growth and increasing resource demands: world population will be more than 9 billion and the demand of livestock products will surpass the number of population growth. Through these changes, the livestock sector has a more direct rivalry for scarce resources such as land, water and energy. Consequently, livestock sector's evolution is more and more related to world food security due to the conflict between food destined to fodder and food for human consumption.

However, with the current technological development it is possible to resolve the deficiencies in the marginal regions and, in this way, avoid the impact livestock production can have in those areas. Although future demand in food and commercial crops will grow slower than before, satisfying this demand will still require the continued expansion of farming lands together with the improvement in performance based on new vegetal varieties and farming technologies [FAO, 2006b].

However, I consider it necessary to ask ourselves some questions:

• Are there suitable amounts of water and land enough to enlarge the farming and grazing surfaces? Or are these vital resources in short supply?

• Is there a margin to obtain higher agricultural performance? Or are we reaching the maximum soil exploitation?

• Can biotechnology provide a new crop generation suitable for the environment and greater performance?

• And lastly, are there any plans for agriculture to be able to increase production while improving ecosystems conservation?

Personally I share Mia McDonald's view, Executive Manager at Brighter Green, who mentions that "there is no way to hunger and malnutrition can be eradicated, or equity achieved, if we continue to use more than 30% of the Earth's *land surface and 70% of agricultural land for livestock and feed production"* [Global Forest Coalition, 2013].

# Chapter 3

# Environment

*Translation: Fátima Madonna*

## 3.1 Appetite for meat as the driving force behind environmental damage

In parenthesis, I would like to say that, in my opinion, this is the most relevant issue under consideration. We are totally dependent on nature: we extract all the resources from nature to satisfy our basic needs. If we want to succeed as species, we should reconsider our relationship with the environment, since we are about to reach the point of no return, where no matter what we do, it will be too late to make up for the inflicted damage incurred [Butzer, 2012].

In order to make an analysis on this statement, it is necessary to know the available facts and information (which, by the way, are a lot).

Due to the progress made in environmental science, it has come to light that the human appetite for meat is one driving force behind almost every environmental phenomenon that threaten the future of human life: deforestation, erosion, fresh water scarcity, climate change, loss of biodiversity, social inequality, destabilization of communities, and the spread of diseases [Subak, 1999; Steinfeld *et al*, 2006; Nguyen *et al*, 2010; UNEP, 2010; Scientific American, 2011, Capper, 2011].

The current threats to biodiversity have no precedents. At the moment, the loss of species is estimated to be between 50 and 500 times higher than the loss registered throughout the history of the planet [Baillie *et al*, 2004]; some previous authors suggest it is even higher [Wilson, 1989]. By the year 2005, 15 out of 24 ecosystems that supply important environmental services were in decline [MEA, 2005].

In 306 out of 825 terrestrial ecoregions identified by the World Wildlife Fund, which contain all the biomes and biogeographic communities, the livestock sector is currently a threat. International Conservation has identified 35 critical places in the world. These places are characterized by having exceptionally high levels of plant endemism, and serious levels of loss of habitats: 23 out of these 35 places are affected by livestock production [Steinfeld *et al*, 2006]. An analysis of the Red List of Threatened Species from the International Union for Conservation of Nature and Natural Resources shows that most of the threatened species in the world are prone to the loss of habitats due to livestock activity [UICN, 2013].

Despite all the efforts to minimize the destruction of

tropical forests and to protect natural ecosystems, upcoming years do not seem hopeful about conservation of forests and biodiversity. Classical approaches to conservation, such as the attempt to preserve pristine nature inside national parks and other protected areas, have failed to stop the spread of their degradation [Contestabile, 2012].

But let's go step by step.

## 3.2 Deforestation

### 3.2.1 Forests disappear

Nowadays, deforestation is an environmental problem concerning a lot of people. It has often been heard about campaigns against deforestation and logging mounted by groups of people, governmental institutions and non-governmental organizations [Brown & Zarin, 2013]. Deforestation is a hot topic among environmental issues.

To care about deforestation is completely reasonable and obvious. We have been taught at school that we should take care of forests because they are important for us: they interchange carbon dioxide for oxygen [NRC, 2013]; they protect the soil from desertification and help with soil recovery [UNCC, 2013]; they function as fresh water storage of drinking water [CIFOR, 2012; FAO, 2013]; they are home for millions of species of flora and fauna [WWF/ZSL/GFN, 2010]; they constitute educational and learning environments; and they are a source of easily available resources [FRA, 2010]. There exist a lot more reasons. It is not possible to summarize the importance of forests in a few words; they have an enormous impact on our daily lives, even on thouse of us living in noisy and crowded places. Despite our dependency on these ecosystems, we allow their depletion.

Ten thousand years ago, after the last glacial era, 45% of the Earth's surface was covered with woods and forests [FRA, 2010]. Nowadays, 31% of the Earth's surface is covered with forests (about 9 billion hectares) [FRA, 2010], and since 1950, we have deforested more than ever [Callahan, 2001].

### 3.2.2 Forests and humankind

Forests have played an important role in the history of humankind. Regular deforestation has eased population growth by the years. Throughout time, the interaction between humans and forests has been changing in response to social and economic contexts; there are no doubts about the relationship among the use of forests, the socioeconomic development, and the destruction of forests (with the succeeding environmental damage), and the following economic decline [FAO, 2012].

Deforestation is understood as the removal of a forest or stand of trees where the land is thereafter converted to a non-forest use [SFA, 2008]. For a period of 5000 years, the accumulated loss of forests around the world was 1.8 billion hectares, that is, 360 thousand hectares per year [Williams, 2002]. Population growth and the succeeding great demand of food, fibre, fuel, and other resources accelerated the process, and consequently, the average annual loss of forests became 5.2 million hectares per year, in the last 10 years [FRA, 2010].

The oldest evidence of deforestation dates back to the Mesolithic period (around 10 thousand years ago). It was a small-scale practice by some societies with the aim to make closed forests into open ecosystems that would enable hunting [Brown, 1997]. The first sedentary farmers (primitive farmers) that settled permanently in Europe, around 4500 B.C. were the ones who made significant deforestation [Williams, 2000]. They seem to have practiced primitive agriculture based on logging and slash-and-burn technique using stone and silex axes, in large extensions of forests to clear more land for cultivation [Clarck, 1947; Williams, 2000].

As agriculture spread out, humans cleared the fields of trees and bushes to make it suitable for agriculture, livestock herding, urbanization and irrigation. Since 3000 B.C. approximately, until the end of medieval times, the increase of population growth brought about big changes in the vegetation of forests in Europe and China [Williams, 2000].

By the end of the 18th century, in Great Britain, a clever man named James Watt decided to improve the Newcomen machine, which had been developed some years before. His improvement resulted in the first steam machine: one of the driving technologies of the First Industrial Revolution [Kreis, 2001]. In the social sphere, a ripple effect begun: increase in agricultural productivity and, consequently, in food offer; technological improvement and industrial growth; rural-urban migration; improvement of sanitary conditions; increase in salaries and income, thus, in consumption which led to economic growth [Homer & Sloan, 1982].

The preceding facts led to an unprecedented increase in population. At that time, the population of Great Britain and Wales was around 6 million people, but when the 19th century begun, population grew to 8.3 million, and by 1950 to 16.8 million [GB Historical GIS, 2009]. In 1750, the world was populated by approximately 750 millions of people, increasing up to 1 billion in 1804, 2 billion in 1927, 3 billion in 1960, 4 billion in 1974, 5 billion in 1987, 6 billion in 1999, and 7 billion in 2012 [UN, 1999; World Meters, 2013].

This increase in population caused many impacts on forests. Historically, deforestation has been more intensive in areas further from the equator than in tropical regions. However, in the last 50-100 years the situation has changed, and deforestation rates are now higher in tropical countries.

### 3.2.3 Increase in consumption of animal source foods

Livestock has been (and still is) an important factor in the growth of global agriculture. Global food economy is being increasingly driven by the change in the consumption patterns of livestock products. This trend is termed 'livestock revolution' by some [Delgado et al, 2001].

As I mentioned in the first chapter, livestock production rapidly grew as the result of a growing demand of animal products, and since 1960, global meat production tripled, milk production almost doubled, and egg production has grew almost four times.

The following table summarizes the discussion in Chapter 2.7 on the increase in meat consumption since 1950.

| Year | Global meat production (tons) | Consumption: Kg/person/year |
|---|---|---|
| 1950 | 44 millon | 17,2 |
| 1970 | 100 millon | 27,08 |
| 2002 | 242 millon | 39 |
| 2007 | 285,7 millon | 45,71 |
| 2013 | 308,3 millon | 44,03 |
| **2050 (estimaded)** | **455 millon** | **49,4** |

*3.2.4 Deforestation = Meat consumption?*

Global meat production has grown 25 times since 1800 [Galloway *et al*, 2010], with an increase in the occupation of natural ecosystems for grazing and feed-crop production. The conversion of natural habitats into pastures and cropland has been a rapidly growing trend, with a great acceleration since 1850 [Goldewijk & Battjes, 1997]. However, between 1950 and 1980, more land has been turned into cropland than in the previous 150 years [MEA, 2005].

This shows the great effects of meat consumption on deforestation, because its production requires large extensions of land. The surface of the earth occupied by livestock systems is estimated in 26% and 45% [Steinfeld *et al*, 2006; Thornton *et al*, 2011]; the great majority of them correspond to lands previously occupied by forests, savannah, and native pastureland.

Commonly, deforestation begins with the construction of roads through forests, opening them up to logging and mining.

Once forests are cleared along the roads, commercial or subsistence farmers start crop production. But the soils of forests have low availability of nutrients and are too fragile to sustain crops for a long time [Swift *et al*, 1998]. After two or three years, soils are depleted, production decreases, and farmers leave and move to other lands. Consequently, livestock producers arrive. A small investment is needed to start livestock production in cheap or abandoned grasslands. Profits can be high, at least for a while, until 5-10 years later, when the excessive grazing and the loss of nutrients turn lands, which used to be storage of biodiversity, into sterile fields [FAO, 2006].

In 2004, pastureland was two thirds of the total of global agricultural land; just one third was used for crops. Of the total of cropland, one third was used for feed [Asner *et al*, 2004].

The advance of the agricultural frontier is higher in meat-producing countries, which are affected by deforestation. In Latin America, for example, almost all cleared land was turned into pastures for livestock in extensive grazing systems. In this territory, the conversion of forests is mainly subjected to the creation of pastures and cropland, no matter the characteristics of the soil, rainfall, climate, or topography. Pastures occupy the major part of agricultural lands in the region, and generally, livestock profitability, as a business, is low [FAO, 2006]. However, the activity becomes profitable if land occupation is guaranteed.

In 2006, Greenpeace International made a very complete report on deforestation in the Amazon called "Eating up the

Amazon", explaining the expansion of soybean cultivation over the forest and how this soybean production ends up for export as feed for livestock that, later on, becomes the raw material of fast food chains and supermarkets [Greenpeace, 2006]. As it seems not to have had much impact in the Brazilian state, in 2009, Greenpeace Brazil published a report in the World Social Forum of Belem, which shows that up to 80% of the deforestation in the Amazon forest results from the increase in breeding stock for human consumption. The report titled "Amazon Cattle Footprint, Mato Grosso: State of Destruction" shows the direct relationship between the expansion of livestock systems and deforestation in the state of Mato Grosso — the area in the Amazon that has the highest deforestation rate [Greenpeace, 2009].

Since I do not support Greenpeace, and I have no intentions of promoting them, I will cite other authors that have come to the same conclusions. Nepstad and colleagues assert that the extensive livestock system is responsible for 80% of deforestation in the Amazon and that 74 million heads of cattle that existed by 2008 occupied 84% of the lands for grazing systems [Nepstad *et al*, 2008]. May and colleagues estimated that 15% of Legal Amazon in Brazil (region including 9 states of this country) have been converted for farming and livestock activities, most of which corresponds to pastures for grazing [May *et al*, 2010]. Previous studies have also explained that pastures for grazing correspond to 60-70% of recently cleared lands [Margulis, 2004; Wassenaar *et al*, 2007].

This data is developed in a report from the Swedish Institute for Food and Biotechnology, where it is mentioned that during 2006, only 5% out of the total livestock population in Brazil (around 175 million of heads of cattle) was bred in feedlots and that pastures were the dominant feed system [Cederberg *et al*, 2009].

The region of Legal Amazon in Brazil occupies approximately 500 million hectares, from which 400 million hectares originally corresponded to forests. By 2003, around 65 million hectares were cleared: a 16% of original forests [Fearnside, 2005]. Soares-Filho and colleagues estimated that if current trends of farming expansion continue, by the year 2050, approximately 40% of forests in the Amazon Basin will be removed [Soares-Filh *et al*, 2006].

And it seems this will happen. The report "Projections of Agribusiness 2008/2009 to 2018/2019" published by the Department of Agriculture from Brazil, mentions the intention of increasing twice their meat production and becoming its main exporter by the year 2018 [Morin, 2008]. Such development will have great repercussions, not only over the carbon emission rates but also over the loss of biodiversity and the maintenance of the cycle of water in the Amazon; it is estimated that more than 70% of the forest cover from the Amazonic ecosystem is needed to maintain the rainfall regime [Soares-Filho *et al*, 2006].

I emphasize that the soil sustaining the tropical forests is not too fertile, and it does not supply better pastures or crops. However, the expansion of livestock into tropical and subtropical forests results from the cheap or even free availability of recently cleared lands, the low efficiency of land use for crops, and the fact that there are only few animals per hectare [McAlpine *et al*, 2009; Bowman *et al*, 2012]. The most important way for direct conversion of tropical forests into pastures is wildfires [Maarten Dros, 2004].

Therefore, deforestation aiming to create pastures can be profitable despite the inefficiency of soil regarding the amount of feed produced. Adversely, tropical forests have been – and still are – the main source of agricultural lands [Gibbs, 2010].

In any case, conversion of tropical forests into pastures is not the only way of deforestation. By the end of 1990 and beginnings of 2000, soybean cultivation, used at a large scale as feed, has also extended rapidly in the Amazon Basin being responsible for one fourth of the total amount of deforestation [Morton *et al*, 2006]. Between 1994 and 2004, the surface destined to soybean cultivation in Latin America doubled and exceeded 39 million hectares. This trend mainly results from the great increase in the demand of livestock products, which caused world meat production to increase three times between 1980 and 2002 [FAO, 2006].

In Central America, during the last four decades, the forest surface has reduced almost 40% simultaneously with an increase in lands for pastures, heads of cattle and forage. It is estimated that between 2004 and 2005, 1.2 million hectares of forests were logged as a consequence of the expansion of soybean cultivation [FAO, 2013].

### 3.2.5 Situation in Argentina

It is not necessary to go to the Congo, Brazil, or Nicaragua to expose this data, since from the total of global forest surface (31%, nearly 4 million hectares), only 12% is protected (460 million hectares) and the remaining 88% is prone to deforestation and bad use [FRA, 2010]. Deforestation is a global phenomenon.

In the report from GEO (Global Environment Outlook) "Environmental Perspectives of Argentina" developed by the National Ministry of Health and Environment of Argentina together with UNEP (The United Nations Environment Program), it can be read: *"Deforestation is identified as the national core problem with the resource of the country, and the maintenance of the productive capacity of forest ecosystems is an essential topic in the strategies struggling against this process"* [GEO, 2004, p95]. Forests in Argentina are among the ones that are disappearing the most.

In the beginning of the 20th Century, there would had been around 100 million hectares of forest in the country. By 1956, this surface had been reduced by half, and the results of the First National Census of Native Forests registered by the Secretary of Environment and Sustainable Development, showed that by 2002, 31.4 million hectares would belong to forest land – only 30% of what existed 100 years ago [UMSEF, 2007].

During the 90s, Argentina occupied the 10th place among the countries with the highest rate of deforestation in the world, with an annual average of 0,88% [FRA, 2010]. Currently, the country has around 30 million hectares of native forest and an annual rate of deforestation of 0,8%, which is higher than Brazil's [FRA, 2010; Hansen *et al*, 2013].

Native forests were subjected to a growing process of deforestation, and big forest regions were converted into agricultural frontiers because of the introduction of unsustainable technologies with high environmental impact. The main factor in deforestation was the availability of lands for livestock and agriculture.

The maintenance of high international prices in the last years has enabled the persistence and even the intensification of the global production of mass consumption products, such as soybean, extending over new lands never before intended for agriculture, because of its low productivity levels in terms of agro-climatic parameters. In this way, soybean cultivation extended from the North of Buenos Aires, Córdoba, and Santa Fe, to provinces like Santiago del Estero, Chaco, Tucumán and Salta, despite climatic constraints (see figure 2, Appendix) [UMSEF, 2012].

The ecoregion that has suffered the most is the "Gran Chaco" (Great Chacho) , which is the biggest forested American ecosystem after the Amazon [Moglia & Gimenez, 1998]. It stretches through Argentina, Paraguay, Bolivia and a little portion of Brazil, embracing 100 million hectares, from which 62,1% is in Argentinean territory (see figure 1 and 3, Appendix). In this ecoregion, more than 3400 species of plants, around 500 species of birds, 150 mammals, 120 reptiles and around 100 amphibians are known; and it is home to approximately 4 million people [TNC/FVSA/DeSdel Chaco/WCS, 2005].

Until the European colonization, the region of "Gran Chaco" was covered with forests that alternate with patches of pastures, making a mosaic maintained by native traditional management, specially through the use of fire as a hunting strategy. This balance between woody and herbaceous vegetation was altered when the European conquerors occupied the territory introducing livestock and selective logging of forests. Consequently, establishing cattle and equine stock in the wild constituted a major event in the modification of the system in Chaco. When pastures and forests entered a process of depletion, pens were replaced by sheep and gout [Cabido *et al*, 2005]. Recently, technical improvements in livestock systems and the expansion and intensification of agriculture, have intensified the deforestation process in the region of Chaco [Zak & Cabido, 2004].

In the rest of the country, deforestation was also triggered by the advance of the agricultural frontier. The extension of cultivated land shifted from 2.4 million hectares in 1888, to 27.3 million hectares in 1943: the expansion of the agricultural frontier was at the expense of the forest [UMSEF, 2007]. Since the 70s, *"Cerealización"* (cerealization) began in the Pampa Húmeda (humid pampa - see figure 3, Appendix), and livestock exploitations were pushed towards marginal zones with worst agricultural conditions. In the 90s, deforestation was used at a large scale to incorporate new lands into more profitable activities, such as livestock, and grain production, especially soybeans [INDEC, 1988-2002]. It is in this decade that an unprecedented process of deforestation began, benefited by technologic changes as direct seeding, or the incorporation of genetically modified crops, and by Chinese markets opening to international trade, in the international context. The main negative environmental impacts on agricultural lands were caused by the agricultural model that encouraged the use of specific crops, technology, and machinery without considering ecologic conditions of the region, like monsoon climate and the fragility of the soil. As a consequence of that, after some years of intensive farming, soil erosion was evident and the decrease in the productivity of crops caused farmers to leave those lands [Boletta *et al*, 2006].

According to Hansen and his colleagues, between 2002 and 2012, the loss rate was higher in dry forests of South America than in tropical forests because of the great deforestation in the forests of Gran Chaco [Hansen *et al*, 2013]. Therefore, the annual deforestation rate of Argentina during 2006-2011 was 1,22% [UMSEF, 2012] — much higher than the world average (0,13%), the annual rate of Africa (0,49%) or the annual rate of Central America (1,19%) [FRA, 2010].

Next, I will quote some paragraphs of the article "Territorial singularities and environmental problems of an asymmetric country in terminal decline" written by Prof. Jorge Morello, PhD, (deceased) and Silvia Diana Matteucci, PhD, published in Realidad Económica from Instituto Argentino para el Desarrollo Económico (Economic Reality, magazine by the Argentinian Economic Development Institute) in 2000, that straightforwardly explains the problems with the situation of forests in Argentina [Morello & Mateucci, 2000]:

> *"Another valuable resource of our country has been forests, which have suffered a great loss of surface, from 425.000 km2 (in times before colony) to an average of 280.000 km2 in 1992. In that period, woody vegetation, including forests, bushy formations, and bushy steppes that covered 61,4% of the territory, reduced to 36% in the same period. To this, it must be added that the remaining forest lands are in a variable state of decline. The basic reason of this situation is the potential of multiple uses of forest lands. 65% of lands from native forests have a potential use for farming; 85% of native forests have a potential and actual use for livestock. The loss of resources from forests took place due to the advance of livestock, forest, agricultural and forestry exploitation."*

> *"[...] Hill livestock farming has been practiced since colonial times for cattle, sheep and gout. The use of fire for clearing has been massively used in Chaco and in forests from the region of The Andes and Patagonia. In Chaco, fire was used in the pre-Hispanic period by ethnic groups from Chaco for purposes of hunting, better visibility, communication, fighting, and cleaning the land for corn and yuca farming. Since the beginning of the century, in order to keep the balance between savannah and forest in Chaco, fire, and later, clear-cutting have been used with little or none*

*application. In the South, for more than 150 years, southern forest has been subjected to burns to protect wool produced by sheep. Until 1985, in Tierra del Fuego, forests of Lenga (Nothofagus pumilio) were burned to clear lands for livestock."*

*"[...] The growth of livestock and agriculture in the most fertile lands of Argentina, has not only been disproportionate in relation to other resources of the country, but it has also been very degrading because of the underlying economic rationality. Nowadays, there are more than 9 million hectares in the ecoregions of Pampa and Gran Chaco where dryland farming with high technical improvements (agrochemicals, improved seeds, machinery) is practiced, in a sophisticated model with a strong component of imported supplies and with no introduction of massive irrigation or fertilization. The dominant process that has brought about this current situation began towards the 60s; it was the transition from agriculture and livestock in 12-year rotation to permanent agriculture. Later, there was a shift from predominantly cereal crops to a combination of cereal and oleaginous crops with a current tendency towards exclusive production of oleaginous crops (soybean and canola) twice or three times a year. In semi-arid Chaco, multinational companies are working since 1994 in clearing, land availability, and double cropping."*

*"[...] Hill livestock farming produces damage by*

*lopping for renewal and stripping the barks of old trees; the stock of seeds is reduced by seed predation in species with palatable fruits mainly because damaged trees are less productive of seeds. The result is a deteriorated forest, with distorted trees with low output, and soil compaction by treading. This situation put at risk the possibilities of regeneration of an exploitable forest."*

*"[...] 31% of regional production of meat, wool, and hides, in the Northwest and the Northeast of Argentina is done in bushy formations and forests that simultaneously supply forage, food products, wood, firewood at extraction rates that surpass natural replacement rates."*

Due to this reason, on November 28th 2007, the National Law No. 26.331 of Minimum Budget for Environmental Protection of Native Forests was passed, establishing the minimum budgets for environmental protection to enrich, restore, conserve, take advantage of, and sustainably manage the native forests and the environmental services they supply [InfoLeg, 2007]. Also, a regime of promotion and criteria for the allocation of funds in return for environmental services supplied by forests was established. However, the document published in June 2012 by the Office of Forests of the Department for Environment and Sustainable Development (Dirección de Bosques de la Secretaría de Ambiente y Desarrollo Sustentable - SAyDS), titled "Monitoring of the Native Forests Cover in

Argentina: Period 2006-2011" states: *"The research carried out reveals the existence of deforestation in the period between the passing of the Law No. 26.331 and the passing of the Land Management of Native Forests (OTBN: Ordenamiento Territorial de Bosques Nativos) by each provincial jurisdiction, despite the prohibition of clearing according to the Article No. 8 of the fore-mentioned Law, and the enforcement of the OTBN until the year 2011"* [UMSEF, 2012].

Under this scenario, the Argentinian government has launched the Agri-Food and Agri-Industrial Strategic Plan (Plan Estratégico Agroalimentario y Agroindustrial - PEA) [PEA, 2013], which sets the goals of expansion of agriculture incompatible with the conservation of native forests. The PEA attempts to reach a production of more than 160 million tons of grains (cereals and oleaginous crops) in eight years. A crop of 160 million tons of grain means increasing the total production of cereals and oleaginous crops in more than 50% in relation to 2009/10 crops (100 million tons) and in a 100% in relation to the average production in the last decade.

That increase in production, in any scenario, stands for an expansion of the sown land cover. Under different hypothesis, that expansion oscillates between 9 and 20 million hectares: between 50% and 100% of the remaining area of native forest. We should take into account that the lands where that potential expansion is possible are forest areas [Merenson, 2011].

This has also been mentioned in the report by GEO, but considering a smaller production: *"Additionally, it must be considered that if the country wants to reach 100 million tons in grains, the agricultural frontier should practically be extended between 12 and 15 million hectare; consequently, it could jeopardize the conservation of the current native forest coverage"* [GEO, 2004, p92].

To the above mentioned, we should add the goal of increasing production of bovine meat in a 46%, of poultry meat in an 88%, and of pork meat in a 300% [PEA, 2013].

### 3.2.6 Deforestation in Córdoba

As I mentioned before, the annual deforestation rate of Argentina during 2006-2011 was 1,2% [UMSEF, 2012] – one of the highest in South America; however, the rate is highly surpassed in some areas of the territory such as Santiago del Estero, Salta and Córdoba (see figure 2, Appendix).

The expansion of agriculture has been possible after the conversion of great extensions of forests, which resulted in the disappearance and fragmentation of ecosystems throughout the Centre and North of Argentina, as the case of Córdoba.

In the beginnings of the 20th century, the Province of Córdoba had 12 million hectares of native forest, which have been reduced to 640 thousand hectares relatively well conserved, 1 million hectares of secondary forests, and 960 thousand hectares of scrubland, so that Córdoba was left with less than 10% of its native forests by 2010 [Cabido & Zak, 2010]. The great number of fires and cleared surfaces taking place since that year raises doubts as to whether that high percentage still exists.

In the last years, the forests in the North-West of Córdoba have been the most damaged. Between 1970 and 2000, more than 1 million hectares of forest in Chaco were lost by its conversion into annual crops, mainly soybean. In the 90s, there was a strong advance of clearing and sowing of megathermic exotic pastures for intensive livestock [Britos & Barchuk, 2008]. In the period between 1998 and 2002 the annual deforestation rate in Córdoba was of 2,93%; between 2002 and 2006 it was of 2,5%; and in the last registered period between 2006 and 2011, it was of 1,6% [UMSEF, 2012]. Although it was minimized, it is still too high and cannot be measured against numbers at global level: it surpasses many times the average of global deforestation.

Despite these numbers and the regulatory measures taken to curb the pressure on native forests of the Province of Córdoba, December of 2013 was the month with one of the worst clearing in the last 4 years, making 2241 hectares of native forest disappear [Viano, 2013].

### 3.2.7 Forests in danger, humans in danger

Deforestation is a very serious issue since damage was practically irreversible in cases in which some compensatory action was taken. Forested ecosystems are very fragile and not many people are aware of our great dependency on them. The impacts entailed in deforestation over ecosystems and natural resources are multiple and very important. Among them:

- Reduction of biodiversity (habitat, species and genetic

diversity).

- Loss of biomass.
- An increase of greenhouse effect and global warming, as well as the modification of the cycles of nutrients, specially carbon, since generally biomass is totally burned when clearing.
- Alteration of the hydrologic regime, reduction of the water-holding capacity and the infiltration capacity, modification of surface waters run-offs, reduction of the times of concentration and destabilization of the phreatic zone, which favors flooding or droughts.
- Increase of the erosion and sedimentation of the soil, as well as of the possibility of soil loss because of the increase of natural phenomena of massive removal (mudslides).
- Migrations of animals that, in the case of endemic species, may provoke the extinction of other species.
- Increase of poaching and illegal commerce of wood.

At the same time, the loss and deployment of forestal resources significantly affects the life quality of native population that have supported or complemented their subsistence with forestal resources as a source of food or commercial supply.

In such cases, the loss of native technologies and cultural uses, causing migration to urban centers with the corresponding social and economic costs, as well as the loss of cultural values and ancient practices take place. On another level, it should be highlighted that economic loss can be registered because of the disappearance of recreational and touristic areas, and the activities developed from the attractive forests.

## 3.3 Water Usage

### 3.3.1 The importance of freshwater

Water is a basic natural resource for all ways of life on earth, and it is a crucial resource for humankind. Sources of freshwater provide for a wide range of goods such as water suitable for irrigation.

Also, water is essential for natural ecosystems and climate regulation. The continuous movement on the earth surface, over and under the earth, as liquid, steam or ice is called hydrologic cycle. The process of evaporation, particularly from the oceans, is the primary mechanism of the stage "from the earth surface to the atmosphere" in the cycle. Evaporated water returns to the ocean and masses of water through rain [USGS, 2013].

Despite the total amount of water present on earth is relatively constant over time, its availability is scarce and it results particularly exposed to climate change. Only 2,5% of all water resources corresponds to freshwater, while oceans amount to 96,5%, and salty water amounts to 1% (other saline water). Moreover, almost 70% of all freshwater resources are trapped in glaciers, in eternal snow, and in the atmosphere.

Scientists warn that in the next century, accessibility to

water could reduce due to climate change that could trigger an alteration in the rainfall regime. This fact will cause the reduction of available water for irrigation, and consequently, for food production [Unión Europea, 2011].

## 3.3.2 Availability of Freshwater

Water availability has always been a restricting factor for human activities (particularly for agriculture) and the growth in the demand of water is an increasingly worrying factor. Exhaustive extraction and deficiencies in water management have resulted in a fall of phreatic levels damaging the soil and reducing the quality of water all over the world.

In many of the large rivers of the planet, currently, only 5% of the original volumes flows and some of them do not reach the sea during a year [Nuwer, 2011]. The big lakes and continental seas have shrunk and half of the wetland in Europe and North America do not longer exist. Deposits from soil erosion are silting up reservoirs, reducing hydroelectric energy and water supply, while groundwater is being pumped out intensively, and the aquifers are being increasingly more polluted and salinized in coastal regions. All continents are experiencing high rates of degradation of ecosystems related to water [IWMI/SIWI, 2005].

In the beginnings of the 60s, when the green revolution started, the average output of crops in the world was about 1,4 ton/hectare. Thirty years later, in the 90s it increased to about 2,8 ton/hectare, doubling the production due to an improvement in agriculture technology [IWMI/SIWI, 2005]. However, despite having done a great improvement in the comprehension of the nature of water interacting with biotic and abiotic factors to harness its use, pressures over continental water systems are increasing together with demographic growth, economic development and the change in the type of diet.

Nowadays, we are in a planet facing a serious water crisis, which is mainly caused by the way it is used. At the moment, the conditions challenging agriculture are very different from the ones in the 60s: rivers are drying, groundwater is running out, and watching news like "water scarcity" is frequent. Global cultivated land has risen a 12% in the last 50 years (most of them at the expense of forests), and global irrigated lands has doubled during the same period. Consequently, agricultural production has increased between 2,5 and 3 times, and currently it uses 70-80% of all water extractions, with serious consequences for many ecosystems and services we all depend on. Now we know, most certainly, that we cannot longer consider water as an inexhaustible resource [Comprehensive Assessment of Water Management in Agriculture, 2007; FAO 2011].

And, taking into account that demand for food will grow dramatically in this century, with an increasing competency for water, land, and other limited natural resources, to make the best use of all water resources has become a fundamental task.

### 3.3.3 How can we measure the use of freshwater?

The measurement of water use started at the beginnings

of 1990 through the coinage of the term *"virtual water"* by Prof. John Anthony Allan, Ph.D., [Allan, 1993], and it took more than a decade for this concept to gain importance. The importance of the development of this concept awarded him the Stockholm Water Prize in 2008.

Basically, virtual water is the volume of freshwater that, in fact, was used to produce an specific product, that is to say, freshwater used in all the stages of a production chain. This will depend on the conditions in which this process was carried out, including the place and its climatic conditions, and even irrigation efficiency and the methods of production [Hoekstra, 2003].

Virtual water has two important practical applications. The first one is that it is useful as an instrument to assess the security of water resources and the efficiency of freshwater use. The second is that knowing the amount of freshwater needed to produce a specific product, we can get an approximation to the environmental impact that the consumption of that product has. Hoekstra and Hung included the concept 'water footprint' in 2002, to measure the virtual water content accumulated in all goods and services of a production chain, consumed by an individual or a group of individuals in a region [Hoekstra & Hung, 2002].

It is an approximation because water footprint does not measure the seriousness of the environmental impact caused by water consumption and pollution. The environmental impact produced by the consumption of a certain amount of water and its pollution depends on the vulnerability of the local water systems and the total number of consumers and polluters of water.

To measure water consumption is difficult due to the dynamism of the water cycle. Water evaporates from the soil and from the surface of open waters (rivers, lakes, ponds, oceans, etcetera) because of sun and wind power. Besides, plants get water from the soil and release it to the atmosphere through stomas of the leaves, in a process known as transpiration. The evaporation and transpiration processes all together are called evapotranspiration (although in everyday language, the term evaporation generally includes transpiration). Evapotranspiration increases the amount of water in the atmosphere, whereas rainfalls reduce that amount. At the same time, inside the atmosphere, steam moves around in the terrestrial atmosphere according to complex patterns, so that water that evaporates in a place does not necessarily returns as rainfall to the same place. Generally, There is no clear transportation from the oceans to the earth through the atmosphere, since water is transported in return to the oceans through surface waters (rivers, crooks) or groundwater. That is why water on earth remains more or less the same [Hoekstra *et al*, 2011].

Taking into account this fact and that society requires a certain volume of water to satisfy domestic needs – agricultural and industrial – it is very necessary that this requirement does not exceed the replacement rates if we look forward to sustainable development.

In this way, the information about the quality of freshwater available in a certain period of time is granted by hydrologic and meteorological studies, while information about the appropriation of water by humankind through their activities is granted by the water footprint. In this sense, scientists have developed 2 divisions in relation to water used in the processes. Next, I will use the definitions adopted by Hoekstra and his colleagues in 'The water footprint assessment manual: Setting the global standard' [Hoekstra *et al*, 2011]. These are:

1) **Blue water:** it refers to surface freshwater resources (rivers, streams, lakes, wetlands) and groundwater resources (aquifers, phreatic zones). This is the stage in the hydrologic cycle that human beings have tried to modify for their benefit through the construction of structures somewhat conventional, fundamentally canals and reservoirs. The blue water footprint is the volume of surface and groundwater consumed as a result of the production of a good or service, including water used during the process, as well as water that is incorporated into the product or evaporates. This water does not return to the catchment from where it was withdrawn.

2) **Green water:** it refers to the precipitation on land that does not run off or recharges the groundwater but is stored in the soil or temporarily stays on top of the soil or vegetation. Eventually, this part of precipitation evaporates or transpires through plants. Green water can or cannot be made productive for crop growth because there will always be evaporation from the soil and because not all periods of the year or areas are suitable for crop growth. Green water footprint is the volume of rainwater consumed during the production process.

Also, the concept of grey water footprint has been developed. The grey water footprint is an indicator of freshwater pollution that can be associated with the production of a product over its full supply chain. It is defined as the volume of freshwater that is required to assimilate the load of pollutants according to natural background concentrations and existing environmental water quality standards.

It is important to distinguish blue water footprint from green water footprint because hydrologic, environmental and social impacts, as well as the cost of production of surface water and groundwater, clearly differ from those of rain water.

Since the water volume managed is huge, this is expressed in $km^3$/year (cubic kilometers per year). For you to have a point of reference for the following values, you should know that 1 $km^3$ of water equals 1 billion $m^3$ of water, and 1 $m^3$ of water equals a thousand liters of water.

### 3.3.4 Fresh water Use

Thanks to the hydrologic cycle, renewable water resources in the world are about 42 billion $km^3$/year. Only around 3.9 billion $km^3$/year out of that quantity are withdrawn from rivers and aquifers for human consumption (blue water): some 2.71 billion $km^3$ are for irrigation (**70%**), 741 million $km^3$ are for industry (**19%**), and the remaining 429 million $km^3$ (**11%**) are for non-industrial use in communities [FAO, 2011].

Therefore, the agricultural sector is the main consumer of

freshwater. This is because food production is an activity with high levels of water consumption. During the process, great volumes of water evaporate by transpiration of plants or from the soil, irrigation canals and reservoirs. Thus, food production demands 50 to 100 times more water than the amount we use daily at home in domestic tasks (drinking, showering, flushing the toilet, washing clothes) [SIWI, 2012]. This demand has increased globally due to the growth in the demand of products with greater need of water, such as animal source products. Ironically, these preferences for diets are being increasingly adopted in the most populated areas and with more water scarcity.

Assessing the need for water in the future, we should consider how much is needed to feed population at that moment as well as what is needed to eradicate poverty. If we keep water productivity as in the present moment, additional need for freshwater will be of 3.8 billion $km^3$/year in the year 2025, and of 5.6 billion $km^3$/year in 2050 to manage an expected production of 3 billion tons of grains to satisfy industrial and domestic growth. And, taking into account that 3.8 billion $km^3$/year is a very large quantity and corresponds to approximately all actual withdrawals of water to support domestic, industrial, and agricultural needs, we can realize that there is an uncertain situation concerning water resources [IWMI/SIWI, 2005; Alexandratos & Bruinsma, 2012]. It is necessary to contemplate the fact that the increase in the demand of freshwater for non-food uses (industry, cities, biofuels), reduces the availability of blue water for food production. At the moment, the depletion of the water volume in rivers is substantial: 25% of the volume of continental rivers has been depleted; this phenomena is happening mainly in regions where agriculture is dependent on irrigation [Falkenmark & Molden, 2008].

| Year | Total blue water consumption (Km³/year) |
|------|------|
| 2011 | 3900 |
| 2025 | 7800 |
| **2050** | **9500** |

In the year 2011, the global average of water footprint was of 1385 m³/person/year; while in Argentina, that number is slightly over the global average: some 1607 m³/person/year [Makonnen & Hoekstra, 2011]. This is because of the agro-export model of the country, which uses large amounts of water for grain production and livestock products.

The available data about percentages of water use in Argentina during 1993 and 1997 are quite similar to world figures. From a total of 34 thousand m³/year, 24 thousand m3/year was used for irrigation (71%), 4500 m³/year for human consumption, 3 m³/year for direct livestock consumption and 2500 m³/year for industry. However the data of the information system AQUASTAT by FAO corresponding to the year 2000, indicate a change in the percentages: 66,1% corresponds to agriculture, 21,7% to human consumption and 12,1% to

75

industrial use [Arienza *et al*, 2011].

*3.3.5 Water Uses in the Livestock Sector*

We have enough theoretical framework to go into what is of our concern: water use for the production of animal source food.

As already mentioned, in the last 50 years, there has been a growing tendency towards an increase in animal source food consumption (meat, dairy, and eggs), which requires higher amounts of water than other products. Let's see why.

When we talk about water consumption for livestock, it is reasonable to wonder how much water an animal can drink. But, let's remember that water footprint studies water consumption in all the stages of the production process – in this case, of animal source products. And this goes from fresh drinking water for livestock up to water necessary to produce feed (fodder or pastures), and freshwater used in the slaughterhouse.

First, livestock organisms lose water through breathing (lungs), evaporation (skin), defecation (bowels), and urine (kidneys). At the same time, loss of water rises with high temperatures and low humidity. The reduction in water consumption also decreases meat, dairy and eggs production [Steinfeld *et al*, 2006].

Globally, the annual demand of freshwater for direct livestock use is around 16 $km^3$ of blue water [WWAP, 2012]. However, livestock production, especially in industrial farms, also demands water for services such as: cleaning of production units, washing of animals, refrigeration equipment for animals and their products (milk), and waste removal. Particularly, the breed of pigs requires a large amount of water because of the washing system through stream of water (dung is swept along to a canal using large amounts of water, and by gravity, the collected dung is driven to a storage pond). In this case, the need of water for services may be 7 times higher than the need of water for consumption [Hutson *et al*, 2004]. These services add up to 6.5 $km^3$/year of freshwater (blue water) [WWPA, 2012].

Taking into account the 16 $km^3$ of water for livestock direct use, and the 6.5 $km^3$ of water for services, there is a total amount of 22.5 $km^3$/year of fresh water used for livestock. It represents only the 0,6% of total blue water (3900 $km^3$/year). Unfortunately, this number is the only one that is under consideration when drawing up policies; thus livestock sector is not included among the mainly responsible contributors for water resource depletion. However, this number is highly underestimated, since it does not encompass other necessities, direct and indirect, that are implied in livestock production.

Other stage in animal source food production that uses water is the slaughterhouse where water is used, fundamentally, for the cleaning of the building where the slaughtering, evisceration and bone is carried out. Skinning the carcass for leather also requires large quantities of water. In any case, amounts of freshwater used during these processes do not compare to the main source of water use: **fodder production.**

The volume of water use in the production of fodder is

much higher than in the previously mentioned procedures. Remember that 35% of cereals, and 97% of soybean meal globally produced are destined to livestock feed. If we have in mind that agriculture uses 2710 km$^3$/year of blue water (70%), we understand that animal source food production uses lots of water. Percentages of cultivated cereal through irrigation vary largely among high-income countries (38%), middle-income countries (64%), and low-income countries (75%). In low income countries, water use is not devoted to staple, but to fodder and pastures for livestock; these countries have the highest consumption of water because they lack access to efficient irrigation technologies [Frenken & Gillet, 2012].

Even though the amount of water consumption depends on the quantity and the type of animal, and the amount of feed they eat, it is estimated that livestock requires about **2000-3000 km$^3$/year of freshwater (blue water)** [IWMI, 2007].

It should be noted that these values can be applied to mixed and industrial (feed-lot) livestock systems, characterized by high levels of external supplies, such as feed carried through long distances. At the beginning, oleaginous and cereal crops occupy large extensions of fertile land with significant volumes of production, and irrigation used in regions where water is relatively scarce.

For this reason, meat production is very expensive in terms of freshwater requirement. Many authors have described in detail the amount of freshwater needed to produce different kinds of food, including animal source food. Some of them are:

- **Renault y Wallender** estimated that the requirement of freshwater was of 4,3 m³/kg for poultry and of 13,5 m³/kg for beef. While 0,15 m³/kg were needed for vegetables, 0,7-1,4 m³/kg for cereals, 0,45 m³/kg for fruits, 2,5-4,8 m³/kg for nuts and 0,8 m³/kg for milk [Renault & Wallender, 2000].

- The **Stockholm International Water Institute** estimated that the freshwater requirement for meat was of 15 m³/kg; for lamb was of 10 m³/kg; for poultry meat was of 6 m³/kg; for cereals was of 0,4-3 m³/kg; for citric fruits was of 1 m³/kg and for vegetables was of 1,1 m3/kg [IWMI/SIWI, 2005].

- **FAO** estimated that the requirement of freshwater for one head of cattle was of 4000 m³/year; for one head of sheep was of 500 m³/year; for beef was of 15 m³/kg; for lamb was of 10 m³/kg and for poultry meat was of 6 m³/kg. Meanwhile, 1,5 m³/kg were required for cereals; 1 m³/kg for citric fruits; 1 m³/kg for vegetables and 2 m³/kg for palm oil [FAO, 1997]

However, the most complete data is proposed by Water Footprint Network, and it can be confirmed on the website (http://waterfootprint.org). One of the last reports made by its members gave the following estimates regarding freshwater requirements for animal source foods as a result: 15,41 m³/kg for beef; 10,41 m³/kg for sheepmeat; 5,8 m³/kg for pork; 5,5 m³/kg for lamb and 4,32 m³/kg for poultry. In this study, the authors conclude that **the water footprint of any animal**

**source food is larger than the water footprint of plant-source food with equivalent nutritional value** [Mekonnen & Hoekstra, 2012].

### 3.3.6 Long-term Consumption Pattern

Problems related to freshwater scarcity and pollution will worsen in the future because of the rise in the demand of water resources. Many authors have estimated that our dependency on water resources will increase significantly, and this situation will bring about future problems in food security and environmental sustainability [FAO, 2011; SIWI, 2012; OECD, 2012].

As I mentioned before, Millennium Development Goals, established in the Millennium Summit of the United Nations in 2000, aim to reduce the number of malnourished people in the world by half by the year 2015. This goal is intended to be reached in an environmental and sustainable social framework, relatively acceptable, even if reaching that goal involves increasing food production through additional uses of limited resources.

Most regions of the world largely depend on irrigation. Nowadays, 80% of world's water consumption for agriculture directly comes from green water, and the remaining 20% comes from blue water sources [IWMI, 2007]. It is at this moment that future problems about food production emerge: groundwater and river depletion due to overexploitation because climate change will cause alterations in the rainfall regimes; consequently, we must resort to blue water even more for food production. Besides, the expansion of and dependency on groundwater have grown over time, many times making irrigation problems worse. Indeed, in the last 50 years, groundwater depletion has doubled, and now, it is of 300 km$^3$ per year [SIWI, 2012].

One thing is clear: current patterns of food production are untenable in that they imply overexploitation of groundwater on a large scale, river flow rate depletion, and damage to aquatic biodiversity. We must add environmental deterioration and loss of production potential caused by water pollution with chemical and agricultural products, eutrophication and salinization of water resources.

For this reason, many studies have been carried out to analyze the security of water resources in the future, and to technically back up the development of policies towards that direction. Studies have been focusing on the impact that climate and economic change will have on the availability of water [Arnell, 2004; Milly *et al*, 2005; Fung *et al*, 2011]. However, a few of them have analyzed the impact of dietary preferences on the availability of water resources.

The first study in relation to that was done by Renault and Wallender in 2000. They classified 5 types of diets in relation to the amount of animal source food they contained. The analysis resulted that water requirement, according to consumption patterns in California by 2000, was of 5,4 m$^3$/person/day (43% of animal source products), while a reduction of 25% in animal products would require 4,6m$^3$/person/day, and a vegetarian diet only 2,6 m$^3$/person/day [Renault & Wallender, 2000].

The University of Stockholm (Stockholms Universitet)

together with Potsdam Institute for Climate Impact Research (PIK), carried out a series of studies intended to assess water availability for crops by 2050. The analysis showed that there will not be enough available water in croplands to produce food for the number of population expected by 2050 if we keep current trends towards diets rich in animal source food (3000 kcal/day out of which 20-30% corresponds to animal source proteins). However, it is mentioned that there will be enough water if the proportion of animal source food is restricted to the 5% of the total calories [SIWI, 2012].

More recently, Vanham and colleagues made an analysis of the diets in Europe and of its water footprint; it resulted that the vegetarian diet had the lowest levels of water footprint, and that reduction of animal source food consumption was followed by a reduction in water footprint [Vanham *et al*, 2013]. Recently, Ercin and Hoekstra showed again how water footprint can change in a significant way if the consumption pattern slightly changes towards a diet with fewer animal source products [Ercin & Hoekstra, 2014].

Food production must be unfailingly sustainable in relation to resource management. A change in consumers' preferences will increase the demand of products that need less water for production, and farmers will simply respond. This will have a great effect on the demand of water and food security.

## 3.4 Water pollution and watershed degradation

### 3.4.1 Livestock sector as a source of water pollution

Here the analysis is harder since water depletion due to

pollution is not quantifiable. But, the contribution of the livestock sector to the process of pollution has been clearly shown in the studies carried out in the U.S.

We now that the major part of freshwater and water used for livestock services returns to the environment as dung or sewage. Industrial farms, that are huge farms (also known as feedlots), provide space for thousands of cows, chickens, or pigs, and produce large amounts of animal waste. The way this waste is stored and used has profound effects on human health and the environment. Livestock excrement contains considerable quantities of nutrients (nitrogen, phosphorus, and potassium), remains of medicine, heavy metals and pathogenic microorganisms. If these reach water or accumulate in soil, they can pose a serious threat to the environment and human beings [Gerber & Menzi, 2005]. Thus, water pollution can be caused through direct runoff from stables, losses in filtrations in storage, livestock waste in sources of freshwater, and drainage that allows deep infiltration and transportation through soil layers.

To understand what has been said, it is necessary to know that in most of these farms, animals are crammed in relatively small spaces with high population density; thus, manure and urine are discharged through runoff or washing systems into storage lagoons. These do not represent, exactly, a blue mirror, but they are great holes in the soil, full of animal waste; some of them are bigger than 7 hectare, and they can contain from 75 to 170 million liters of sewage [NRDC, 2013a]. This large amount of sewage in small areas is so because, for instance, a dairy cow produces approximately 54 kg of wet manure a day, equivalent to 20-40 people's feces [EPA, 2004].

Frequently, water contained in lagoons is withdrawn for land irrigation. Even though manure can be an excellent fertilizer when applied to rates that can be absorbed by crops, industrial farms produce a lot more manure than the amount the soil can absorb, leading to waste leaching into groundwater.

It is not difficult to assume that there is a wealth of opportunities for disaster, since these lagoons frequently break, leak, or spill if they are overloaded, and they can cause a dangerous release of microbes resistant to medicine and of residual nutrients, such as nitrogen and phosphorus. For example, in 1995 there was a spill after the collapse of a pound containing manure from pigs, and 94 million of liters were discharged into New River [NYT, 1995]. In 1999, when hurricane Floyd lashed North Caroline, at least 5 lagoons containing manure were broken [NRDC, 2013b]; and in 2011, a farm of pigs in Illinois spilled 750 thousand liters of manure into a stream killing more than 110 thousand fishes [SJR, 2011].

Those are some examples we can find.

*3.4.2 Eutrophication and dead zones*

Livestock manure contains high concentrations of nutrients, such as nitrogen and phosphorus. Steinfeld and colleagues estimated that, globally, in 2004, livestock excreta contained 135 million tons of nitrogen and 58 million tons of phosphorus. These numbers show that cattle is mainly responsible for the discharge of nutrients with a 58% corresponding to nitrogen, while pigs were responsible for 12%, and poultry for 7% [Steinfeld *et al*, 2006]. In countries where environmental regulations are weak or do not exist, manure is continually applied directly to the soil, exceeding the capacity of the land to assimilate the nutrients. This overload of nutrients can surpass the absorption capacity of local ecosystems and degrade the quality of surface water and groundwater.

Consequently, algae and microorganisms bloom causing eutrophication, bad taste and smell in water, and excessive bacterial growth in systems of distribution. Also, microorganisms can be protected from the effects of temperature and salinity, posing a risk for public health [EPA, 2004].

Eutrophication is a natural process in old lakes and estuaries; but livestock and other agricultural-related activities can largely accelerate the rate of nutrients and organic substances swept along by surrounding drainage basins, and discharged into the aquatic ecosystems. If the growing of plants stimulated by eutrophication is moderate, the result may be a nutritious basis for aquatic communities. However, if it is excessive, the proliferation of algae and microbial activity can cause a rise in the consumption of oxygen and alter the normal functioning of the ecosystems [Chislock *et al*, 2013].

This process is current in freshwater ecosystems as well as in marine ecosystems where the proliferation of algae causes problems releasing toxic substances and provoking anoxia and hypoxia because of oxygen consumption. Thus, dead zones are created, with great negative impacts on aquaculture and fishing.

Organic matter, which derives from the organisms' excreta and natural decay, is degraded for future reuse by bacteria; during this process in the food chain, oxygen is consumed. However, when the amount of organic matter increases artificially because of the discharge of waste into agricultural and industrial waters, bacterial population also increases; at the same time, the consumption of oxygen dissolved raises more than three times its normal value. This negative process gives rise to a steep reduction of this vital gas, and triggers a significant mortality of living organisms that constitute the ecosystem [Diaz & Rosenberg, 2008].

There are several dead zones in the world, but one of the most well-known ones studied by its extension and alarming state, is the dead zone of the Gulf of Mexico on the mouth of Mississippi river in front of the coasts of Louisiana and Texas; according to scientists from the University of Texas A&M, the zone extended 8500 km$^2$ around the year 2011 [NOAA, 2011]. However, the drainage basin of the Mississippi River occupies the third place in the world, after the Amazon and Congo Rivers, because of its size – the percentage of drainage is around 41% of the U.S. territory.

### 3.4.3 Biologic pollution

The bad disposal of livestock waste causes biologic pollution of waters, since livestock excretes a lot of zoonotic microorganisms and multicellular parasites of great significance for human health. Even though an effective transmission needs big amounts of pathogens directly discharged, a lot of biologic pollutants can survive days, and, sometimes, weeks in excretions spread over the field. In this way, they can reach groundwater through soil infiltration. Some of the relevant pathogens, we can find Campylobacter *spp.*, Escherichia coli, Salmonella *spp.*, Clostridium botulinum, Giardia lamblia, Cryptosporidium parvum, Microsporidia *spp.*, Fasciola *spp.* and other microorganisms [Hudson, 2008].

The above mentioned can be dangerous for public health, not only because of the possibility of infection and subsequent disease, but also because of the building up of microbial resistance to antibiotics. This happens due to the fact that large amounts of antibiotics are used in the livestock sector with different purposes. For example, they are given to animals with therapeutic purposes, but they are also given to groups of healthy animals for prevention, and fundamentally, during stressful situations with high risk of infection, such as at weaning or when transported. These compounds are given routinely with food and water during long periods of time to enhance growing rates and feed conversion ratio [Steinfeld *et al*, 2006]. An important part of the medicine used does not degrade, and ends up in the environment, that is way antibiotic waste has been identified in several aquatic environments, from groundwater to tape water.

The previous facts contribute to the increase of bacteria resistance to antibiotics generated due to low concentrations of them, which produces a selective pressure on water. So antibiotic-resistant bacteria will keep breeding and transmitting the genes for resistance to other microorganisms, pathogenic and non-pathogenic, through transference of plasmids (genes transmitted from one bacterium to another) [Oppegaard, 2001].

A great deal of evidence shows that there is high resistance to antibiotics in bacteria associated to animals that were given antibiotics without therapeutic purposes. This resistance spreads to other animals and humans, directly through contact, and indirectly through food chain, water and soil [Marshall & Levy, 2011]. The problem of public health is such that reliable scientific organisms as the Center for Livable Future from John Hopkins University, are claiming the U.S. Food and Drug Administration (FDA) for the removal of antibiotics for non-therapeutic use, since farmers use around 70% of the total of commercialized antibiotics in that country [Science, 2013].

In Argentina, the absence of regulations on that subject leads to a lack of motivation to study these facts. However, a research carried out by Chagas and colleagues in 2006 found positive results when analyzing possible pollution on rivers and sediments accumulated in the lowest zones of the drainage basin of Tala creek and neighboring creeks, located in the Undulated Pampa* (located 160 km to the Northwest of the capital of Argentina, Province of Buenos Aires). As result of the analysis, there were found high concentrations of biologic indicators of animal-source pollution (groups of faecal streptococcus and enterococcus) [Chagas *et al*, 2006]. It should be noted that the Undulated Pampa is a region of growing agriculturalization with predominance of extensive and intensive livestock (grazing and feed-lot, respectively), and

---

*The soft waves that characterize the land of this area gave rise to its name, Undulated Pampas. The soils on these plains are among the most fertile in the world. This fertility, together with the mild weather conditions typical of the area, enabled the growth of cereal-growing belts in this area of Argentina as well as in similar latitudes in the northern hemisphere.

significant water erosion. To this situation, it must be added that farmers lack information about the negative impacts of their activities upon surface water and groundwater, as shown in some studies done in the Province of Buenos Aires [Nossetti *et al*, 2002; Sardia *et al*, 2012].

Other ways of water pollution on the part of the livestock sector are heavy metals used in low doses for health reasons and breeding enhancement. Thus, other pollutants come from sewage from slaughterhouses with great loads of fat, blood and sediments, and from agrochemicals in the production of fodder [EPA, 2004; Steinfeld *et al*, 2006; Hudson, 2008].

### 3.4.4 Legal regulation

Unlike the United States, Canada, or any European country, where the enforcement and observance of specific regulatory frameworks for management and use of livestock excreta exist, in Argentina, there are no specific norms in relation to manure management. However, there are provincial laws, such as the Act on protection of sources of supply, of watercourses and waterbodies, and of the atmosphere, that in the Province of Buenos Aires regulates all kind of discharge of residual effluents (soli, liquid or gas) from any origin that can degrade the quality of air or water [Pinos-Rodriguez *et al*, 2012]. The decree 2009/60 regulates this Act and establishes that local governments are responsible for inspections and impositions of fees [GBA, 2009]. Nevertheless, this regulation does not apply to the rest of the country.

## 3.4.5 Degradation of watershed*

The livestock sector, apart from contributing to the use and pollution of water resources, also causes a direct impact on the process of water recharge through soil degradation. Excessive grazing and the mechanic action of hoofs on soils can produce great disturbances in the function of pastures and the water cycle in riverbanks, since they affect water infiltration and retention, and the morphology of the flow [USFWS, 2009].

High water basins, in which upstream flow drains downstream towards low areas and riverbanks, constitute a very serious part of water resources since they play a fundamental role in water quantity and supply. In a basin with good conditions of functioning, most of the rainfall is absorbed by the soil in high lands, and later distributed through the basin by subterranean movements and surface run-off. Any activity that affects the ecologic conditions of high lands will have a significant impact on water resources and riverbank areas. In contrast, riverbank soils are different from highland soils since the first ones are rich in nutrients and organic matter, enabling the retention of large amounts of humidity. The presence of vegetation decreases the speed of the impact of rainfall on earth, and facilitates its absorption, infiltration and the reload of groundwater. Thus, water moves downstream in the subsoil and supplies streams [Barrow, 1998; Brauman *et al*, 2007].

Animals for grazing are an important agent of geomorphological changes. Trampling with hoofs physically

---

*    Part of the next section was extracted from [Heil, 2013].

shapes the land, in addition to the consumption of vegetation that protects the soil, increasing the risk of erosion [Mwendera *et al*, 1997].

The formation of compacted soil layers decreases the levels of infiltration because porosity decreases as well, causing early soil saturation. When there is no infiltration of water, a superficial flow can drain down to infiltrate into another slope or to continue draining until it enters into a stream, eroding and increasing the frequency of floods [Belsky & Blumenthal, 1997; Belsky *et al*, 1999]. In areas around riverbanks, these impacts can be even more dramatic since livestock prefers these areas rather than other because of the easy availability of water, shadow, thermic shelter and varied fresh food. The fact that animals tend to overgraze these areas causes a mechanic imbalance at banks of watercourses and decreases the availability of water at a local level due to the progressive erosion with reduction of the phreatic level and deposition of sediments [Belsky *et al*, 1999].

Erosion caused by livestock in a specific place may spread over the landscape since animals avoid eroded places and look for new feeding areas. Moreover, there may be "contagion" between nearby places, even without animal intervention [Lunt *et al*, 2007], through the spread of land areas cleared of vegetation or through the increase in the depth and extension of gullies.

An example of the aforementioned is the desertification of Sahel region, in the North of Africa, where over-exploitation and inappropriate use of agriculture have caused a great loss of soils with often terrible and dramatic consequences in other regions [Gorse & Steeds, 1987].

This loss of soils is more likely in ecosystems that evolved with few herbivores, while this tendency is less likely in ecosystems that evolved with lots of herbivore animals, where its presence is even necessary. However, high loads of livestock seem detrimental to even the ecosystems that have evolved with herbivores, probably because of the change in the type of livestock [Cingolani *et al*, 2008].

### 3.4.6 Impacts on watershed in Argentina and Cordoba

In Argentina, there are several areas where livestock have had a negative effect on the services provided by water basins due to the great use of grazing lands, specially in pastures from the pampas region (see figure 3, Appendix) [León *et al*, 1984; Sala *et al*, 1986; Facelli *et al*, 1988]. In Patagonia*(see figure 3, Appendix), sheep introduced more than one hundred years ago led to changes in native vegetation with great impact on water balance that resulted in the reduction of the vegetal cover and soil fertility, and changes in plant species [Palacio *et al*, 2014].

But there is an area in which this is stressed and evident; the area is part of one region widely cleared: the Sierras Grandes that are part of the Sierras de Cordoba (mountain range – see figure 4, Appendix).

Particularly, the ecosystem of Sierras Grandes from Córdoba have fragile soils, and erosion easily occurs [Cingolani

---

\* Patagonia is a region located at the southern end of South America, shared by Argentina and Chile. The region comprises the southern section of the Andes mountains as well as the deserts, steppes and grasslands east of this southern portion of the Andes.

*et al*, 2003], so that overgrazing becomes of great significance in the soil degradation of this region.

As I mentioned before, the good condition of the soils of high lands is essential to keep a healthy water basin, and in the Province of Córdoba, Sierras Grandes play an important role in provincial water economy because it encompasses the headwaters of the main rivers and streams that supply freshwater to a large part of the province [Cabido *et al*, 2003; Cingolani & Falczuck, 2003].

From the 17th century, Sierras Grandes have been a place for continuous traditional livestock breeding of high load; since a few years ago, this situation represented a total of 129 thousand hectares (83% of the total surface), with soil conditions showing the greatest degree of degradation and erosion. Some 26 thousand hectares (16,7%) belonged and still belong to the National Park Quebrada del Condorito; this surface suffered a historical exploitation by traditional livestock systems, but since the Park was created in 1997 until today, there has been no livestock system [Cingolani *et al*, 2003].

For frequent visitors to Sierras Grandes, a characteristic landscape caused by unsustainable historic exploitation is the massif of Los Gigantes, where one-meter-depth erosion gullies, or fractions of soil like islands surrounded by erosion can be seen. This scenario largely contributes to the increase in the frequency and intensity of floods in Sierras Grandes, with its subsequent consequences because of soil incapacity for water retention [INA, 2004].

### 3.4.7 Livestock and Tabaquillo

We should add to the above the impact of livestock on tabaquillo forests (*Polylepis australis*). Tabaquillo is a tree, member of the Rosaceae family, that grows at heights between 1200 and 3500 meters above sea level; it is an endemic tree of Argentina, and the southernmost stands are located in Sierras Grandes in Cordoba.

Woodland stands of these trees have the role of 'producing' soil providing fallen leaves that enable the humidity conditions necessary for decomposers to make nutrients available from accumulated organic matter. Thus, the trees also hinder soil erosion through the physical action of retention from their roots. In hydrologic terms, in addition to a more efficiently absorption of rain water during the humid season in soils with an unaltered vegetal structure, foliage from trees also enables mist condensation on its surface that permanently drips and gives water back to woodland soil. This takes place all year long, and the complete process results in a better and more balanced freshwater supply for a wide region by means of small streams that flow into big rivers. **The good state of conservation of these woodlands play a fundamental role in the headwaters of water basins they inhabit; the trees directly take part in the regulation of the water regime resulting in a larger quantity and quality of water** [Renison & Cingolani, 1998; Cabido *et al*, 2003; Robledo *et al*, 2003].

Despite the importance of Polylepsis forests, these are considered as being one of the most endangered forest ecosystems from the neotropic ecozone and in the world because of livestock systems and wildfires [Renison *et al*, 2006; Jameson & Ramsay, 2007].

Particularly, lopping by livestock is one of the main factors determining the survival, growth rate, and structure of forests, and the distribution of tabaquillo mature trees. Although this species have a great capacity to produce new shoots that can even function as a mechanism to stand herbivory, it cannot compensate the impact of high and sustained loads of herbivores [Giorgis *et al*, 2010]. Intensive lopping of new shoots inhibits growth in height, and delays the forestry re-covering after wildfires; thus, tabaquilllo trees are highly consumed and kept in small size [Renison *et al*, 2006].

Since the size of the plant is associated with seed production, this species does not get to compensate the effects of herbivory. There is also another indirect effect of over-grazing on the growth of these trees that delays or inhibits the recovery of forests by means of the deterioration of soils and the subsequent erosion. It is just that trees located in rocky soils can be less productive due to the lack of nutrients and/or water; its growth is remarkably less than trees located in better conserved soils [Suarez *et al*, 2008].

The current state of forests is alarming; to make up this situation, forest recovery is only possible in places where trees that are sources of seeds are not completely cleared, and erosion processes have not yet taken place [Renison *et al*, 2004]. But the re-covering of these lands with forest can be practically impossible if livestock is there [Marcora *et al*, 2013], which is the case of a big proportion of more than 80% of

Sierras Grandes from Cordoba.

### 3.4.8 More livestock systems as the solution?

In general terms, extensive livestock systems are accepted as more compatible with soil conservation than agriculture on large-scale, or urbanization. However, if extensive livestock is compared with the complete elimination of farming activities, as in a protected area, livestock may clearly result as detrimental, relatively neutral, or even desirable for purposes of conservation in ecosystems that evolved with high pressures from domestic or wild herbivores. Then, livestock systems can be compatible with conservation, and even necessary [Lunt *et al*, 2007]. But these changes are not only determined by animals, but also by the particular proneness of soils, its composition, and topography [Cingolani & Falczuck, 2003]. Several recent studies have proposed extensive livestock systems as a solution to desertification and soil erosion. However, these studies were carried out in areas that evolved with high loads of herbivores, where the absence of them results detrimental because of the lack of seed vectors [Sullivan & ClimateWare, 2013]. Thus, the debate around livestock sector as beneficial to the ecosystem will depend on the grazing location.

In places with low productivity that evolved with low loads of herbivory, there is little compatibility between livestock systems and conservation because the loads improving the net profit per units of surface provoke an important loss of vegetal biodiversity.

## 3.5 Global Warming and Climate Change

This might be the most contentious and much debated issue around the impact of livestock on the environment. Therefore, I will try to make the most objective review possible. But first, we should understand what global warming and climate change are.

### 3.5.1 The Atmosphere

The atmosphere is a layer of gases surrounding the Earth, held in place by the gravity of the planet. It is commonly known as "air". The main gases it contains (not counting water vapor) are: Nitrogen (N) 78% and Oxygen (O) 20,95%. There are also other gases found in less amounts, measured in parts per million (ppm), such as: Argon (Ar) 9340 ppm, Carbon Dioxide ($CO_2$) 400 ppm, Neon (Ne) 18,18 ppm, Helios (He) 5,24 ppm, Methane ($CH_4$) 1,7 ppm, Krypton (Kr) 1,14 ppm, and Hydrogen (H) 0,55 ppm [Williams, 2013]. However, this composition varies according to the height at which we are in relation to the differences of pressure.

But the air that makes the atmosphere is more than the air we breathe. The atmosphere is essential for living on Earth because it distributes water. It is part of fundamental processes – such as carbon, nitrogen, and oxygen cycles – and it protects living organisms from damage by radiations and asteroids coming from outer space. These functions are regulated by complex physical and chemical processes that work in a very fragile dynamic equilibrium. Moreover, the atmosphere plays an important role in the Earth's energy balance; in regulating temperature, heat radiated by the Earth is retained and around 30% of solar radiation is reflected towards space [WCRP, 2012]. This is known as Greenhouse Effect, and it consists of a natural phenomenon that occurs in our planet; it has enabled life development, in that it keeps the annual average temperature of the Earth around 15°C instead of -6°C. This mechanism, not simple at all, enables an adequate temperature for life development on Earth, such as we know it; without this mechanism, we probably couldn't live [IPCC, 2007].

Gases responsible for the greenhouse effect are not the most abundant, since nitrogen and oxygen do not have a significant greenhouse effect. Instead, greenhouse effect comes from less common molecules like water vapor, carbon dioxide, methane, nitrous oxide, ozone, among others. In equatorial regions, where there is a lot of water vapor and greenhouse effect is greater, the addition of a small amount of carbon dioxide or water vapor has a minimal direct impact on infrared radiation downwards. However, in dry and cold polar regions, the addition of a small amount of carbon dioxide or water vapor has greater effects. The same happens in the top layers of the atmosphere, which are dry and cold as well [IPCC, 2007].

There are several factors that can alter the concentrations of greenhouse gases in the atmosphere, such as living organisms and oceans. For example, through photosynthesis, plants turn carbon dioxide from air and water into carbohydrates. However, in the industrial era, human activities have added greenhouse gases to the atmosphere, causing global warming [IPCC, 2007].

### 3.5.2 Global Warming Is Real

When talking about global warming, we refer to the unequivocal and continuing rise in the average temperature of the Earth's climate system [IPCC, 2013]. That is, a sustained rise in the temperature of the Earth's surface, including the atmosphere as well as the oceans.

In contrast, when talking about climate change, we refer to all the changes that are arising and may arise in the climate system throughout time as a consequence of global warming. This consists of rainfall regimes' alteration, cold waves, increase in the frequency of hurricanes, etc.

The available data are decisive and the climate models are reliable. In 1988, Prof. Jim Edward Hansen, PhD, introduced one of the first climate models for global warming caused by greenhouse effect gases that included three possible scenarios according to atmospheric concentrations of different gases [Hansen *et al*, 1988]. In 2006, analyzing the model published in 1988, he compared it to the available historical data up to that moment and found that results concerning the rise in temperature were very similar to what had been predicted before [Hansen *et al*, 2006].

The great majority of the most important scientific institutions in the world (for example, NASA [NASA]), asserts the existence of global warming and climate change. To such a level that in 2010, academic societies from most of the industrialized countries signed a statement recognizing the existence of global warming and the urgent need to take measures on that subject. Some of them were: the Brazilian

Academy of Science, the Royal Society of Canada, the Chinese Academy of Sciences, the French Academy of Sciences, the Indian Academy of Sciences, the Science Council of Japan, the Russian Academy of Sciences, the U.S. National Academy of Science, the Royal Society from the United Kingdom, the German Academy of Sciences and the Lincean Academy (Italy) [JSAS, 2010].

However, the most scholarly and recognized institution in the topic is the Intergovernmental Panel on Climate Change (IPCC) established by the United Nations, the World Meteorological Organization (WMO) and the United Nations Environment Program (UNEP). The panel produces reports periodically about global warming and climate change. According to the last report [IPCC, 2013]:

> "Warming of the climate system is unequivocal, and since the 1950s, many of the observed changes are unprecedented over decades to millennia. The atmosphere and ocean have warmed, the amounts of snow and ice have diminished, sea level has risen, and the concentrations of greenhouse gases have increased."

> "[...] Each of the last three decades has been successively warmer at the Earth's surface than any preceding decade since 1850. In the Northern Hemisphere, 1983-2012 was likely the warmest 30-year period of the last 1400 years."

A study published in Science magazine in 2007 analyzed

predictions introduced by the Intergovernmental Panel on Climate Change in 2001 and concluded that: *"Overall, these observational data underscore the concerns about global climate change. Previous projections, as summarized by IPCC, have not exaggerated but may in some respects even have underestimated the change, in particular for sea level"* [Rahmstorf *et al*, 2007].

To conclude and in case there is still any doubt, a recent study that analyzed 11194 scientific articles about anthropogenic global warming in high-academic-level magazines from 1991-2011 found that 97% of scientists studying climate agree that anthropogenic global warming is a fact [Cook *et al*, 2013].

However, despite conclusive evidence about the existence of global warming, there are groups of people (including climatologists) that deny its existence. In 2010, the BBC conducted an interview with Prof. Phil Jones, PhD, director of the Climatic Research Unit (University of East Anglia), where he stated that during the period 1995-2009 global warming was not significant in statistical terms [BBC, 2010], which was taken as evidence by denial groups. Even, there are some groups that put the blame on solar activity for the gradual rise in global temperature; however it has been proved to be a mistake [Schurer *et al*, 2014]. I will also allow myself to say that global warming is not a divine punishment.

It seems that global warming deniers use their political or religious ideology to decide whether to believe or not in the phenomenon, leaving scientific evidence aside or using it deceptively when arguing. Luckily, people from Skeptical Science have done a good job unmasking them [Cook, 2010].

### 3.5.3 Global Warming: Causes

Our awareness of the causes of global warming has raisen over time, and currently, the increase in man-made greenhouse gases is considered as one of the causes [IPCC, 2007]. Since the industrial revolution, the concentration of greenhouse gases in the atmosphere such as carbon dioxide, methane, ozone, chlorofluorocarbon, and nitrous oxide has risen.

Carbon dioxide is the greenhouse gas that contributes the most to global warming, simply because its emissions and concentrations are higher than that of other gases [EPA, 2014].

Methane is the second most important greenhouse gas because it remains in the atmosphere from 9 to 15 years approximately after its emission, and its capacity to retain heat is 21 times higher than carbon dioxide's capacity in a period of more than 100 years. Emissions come from a great variety of sources, both natural and man-made; among them, we can mention landfill sites, oil and natural gas systems, agricultural activities, carbon mines, sewage, and certain industrial processes [EPA, 2014].

Nitrous oxide is the third most important greenhouse gas with the greatest potential for direct global warming because even though it remains in the atmosphere in very small quantities, its capacity for heat retention is 296 times higher than carbon dioxide's capacity, and it remains in the atmosphere for a very long time (114 years) [EPA, 2014].

## 3.5.4 *The Role of the Livestock Sector*

Since it is a controversial topic, and I am not an expert in the area, I will limit myself to expose the information I have found, and I will leave time and science in charge of dispelling the uncertainties.

The contribution of the livestock sector in this process is not deeply nor widely known. Practically in all the stages of the animal production process, substances that contribute to climate change are emitted and released.

In 2006, Steinfeld and colleagues (FAO) published a report called "Livestock's Long Shadow", and one of the chapters concludes that the livestock sector is responsible for 18% of the total anthropogenic greenhouse emissions (measured in equivalence to carbon dioxide), and thus, generating more greenhouse gases than the transportation and industrial sector. This is because 9% of total carbon dioxide emissions, 37% of total methane emissions, and 65% of total nitrous oxide emissions come from livestock sector [Steinfeld *et al*, 2006].

This was measured using LCA technique (Life Cycle Assessment) that makes a detailed assessment of the environmental aspects in relation to all the stages in the life of a product; It is a very useful tool to know the environmental impact of the production of a good or service [SAIC, 2006]. As for the livestock system, it was taken into account not only greenhouse gases from ruminant enteric fermentation and manure, but also the process of land conversion for grazing (deforestation) and fossil fuels burning during cereal production for feed (transportation, tractors, fertilizers, etc.).

103

This has been questioned by some authors who claim that the estimated numbers by Steinfeld and colleagues were inappropriately applied at national and regional levels [Pitesky *et al*, 2009], and that the comparison with the transport sector was quite poor and should be corrected. The authors of "Livestock's Long Shadow" appreciated the corrections and admitted that the comparison was not appropriate [Black, 2010]; but the rumour had already spread, and thus, "Meat Free Monday" was born with the aim of raising consciousness of the population about the role of the livestock sector in climate change. A recently review was done by Sara Place, PhD, and Frank Mitloehner, PhD, in 2012 who also concluded that the estimation of 18% (percentage of greenhouse gases contributed by livestock) was inappropriate [Place & Mitloehner, 2012].

However, according to different authors the participation of livestock in the total emission of greenhouse gases ranges from 10% to 25% [Fiala, 2008; Nelleman *et al*, 2009; Gill *et al*, 2010; Barclay, 2012]. In September 2013, FAO issued a report called "Tackling Climate Change Through Livestock - A Global Assessment of Emissions and Mitigation Opportunities" [Gerber *et al*, 2013], in which it reaffirms the fact that livestock plays an important role in the production of global warming and climate change; although this time, 14,5% of total anthropogenic emissions of greenhouse gases are attributed to livestock. From this number, 41% corresponds to meat production, and 20% corresponds to milk production. This percentage reveals that production and processing of cereals for feed, and enteric fermentation occupy the first place (45% and 39% respectively); while deforestation and burning of fossil fuels were placed in the last positions (20% and 9% respectively). In this way, livestock and animal source food production are on top again.

Carlsson-Kanyama and Gonzalez analyzed the carbon footprint of different dietary patterns, and found that plant foods produce fewer greenhouse gases, while animal source foods have a higher carbon footprint [Carlsson-Kanyama & Gonzalez, 2009]. The study concludes that the decline in meat consumption and increased consumption of plant foods could be an interesting option for the mitigation of global warming and climate change.

More recently, Hedenus and colleagues published a research in the prestigious journal Climatic Change where they make a review on the importance and the need to diminish the consumption of meat and dairy products to help achieve the objectives proposed to mitigate the increase of 2°C expected for the coming years [Hedenus *et al*, 2014]. In another interesting research, Scarborough and colleagues analyzed the emission of greenhouse gases in the diet of 55504 people in the UK and found that those who consumed more than 100 g/day of meat contributed 2.5 times more to greenhouse gases than those who did not eat meat [Scarborough *et al*, 2014]

Moreover, Frank Mitloehner, PhD, participated as a co-author of a study in which it was clear that he had changed his mind in front of the new evidence. In the research it was found that production of calves to sell them as animal destined for meat production represents the stage in the meat production chain in which the greatest amount of greenhouse gases is emitted [Stackhouse-Lawson *et al*, 2012].

### 3.5.5 *What Do We Have To Do?*

The few answers that we have in front of to the imminent global warming are: (1) adaptation to reduce the vulnerability of people and ecosystems to climate change, and (2) mitigation of emissions to reduce the long-term impact of climate change. These must be undertaken jointly, since each of them carried out separately is not enough; however, mitigation is the most important step because it will enable a time-scope for action to achieve adaptation.

The introduction of technological improvements in production processes could be a reasonable alternative because technology is available; though, as usual, it is expensive. Some of them are absurd and obey to the market, such as, the development of a variety of pastures that minimize methane emissions from ruminants [Society of Chemical Industry, 2008]. That will simply contribute to keeping forestal land conversion in regions for livestock grazing.

Other options range from the development of vaccines for ruminants and dietary supplements with synthetic amino acids, to the development of biodigesters for cattle animals* [Gerber *et al*, 2013; INTA, 2013].

Confronted with the lack of economic incentives and state regulations to minimize the greenhouse gases emissions by the

---

*The experimental technique was developed by Argentina's National Institute of Agricultural Technology (INTA), and consists in funneling the digestive gases from bovine stomach cavities through a tube and into a tank.

main responsible sectors, it is hard to imagine how this issue can be solved.

### 3.5.6 What Are We Facing?

Perhaps, global warming as well as climate change are two of the environmental problems we are facing not well known by the general public.

We should understand that it has become an extremely urgent topic. The first decade of the 21st century was the warmest decade registered since 1850 [WMO, 2013], with an average of 0,5°C more than in the period 1961-1990; the years 2005 and 2010 were the warmest.

In November of 2012, the World Bank issued a report warning that we are on path to a 4°C warmer world by 2060, which will have devastating effects on us. Some of them are: extreme heat-waves, declining global food stocks, and life-threatening sea level rise [World Bank, 2012]. This report urges mitigation of global warming and expects global temperature not exceed 2°C rise.

But it is getting late, and we cannot attain the pursued climatic goals. The more we postpone the reduction of greenhouse gases, the more effort we will have to make to stabilize the climate in the planet [Stocker, 2013].

As it is shown in the last report about the emissions of greenhouse gases of different countries from the United Nations Environment Program, actions undertaken until now have not met the requirements. Countries have reduced only one-third of what was needed to avoid a rise of 2°C in global temperature by 2020 [UNEP, 2013].

Perhaps, these temperatures seem minimal for some, but the climate system is complex and delicate, in the sense that a slight alteration could lead to a big disaster. By 2100, it is expected that an increase in the average sea level between 9 and 88 cm, causing floods in low areas, and other damages. Climate zones could suffer a displacement towards the poles, altering forests, deserts and other natural ecosystems. Consequences are serious: the degradation of many ecosystems and loss of species. Furthermore, water resources will also be affected as the result of changes in rainfall regimes and water evaporation [IPCC, 2007].

Direct and indirect effects on economic activities, human settlements and public health will be varied. Poor people and those with limited resources, and more generally, less developed countries will be the most vulnerable facing the negative consequences of climate change, since their capacity for devising mechanisms to approach this situation is more limited than the capacity of developed countries.

# Chapter 4

# *Health*

*Translation: Daniela Lofiego*

## 4.1 Health and Diet

So far we have gone through the inefficiency of the animal source food production model and its impact on the environment.So far we have gone through the inefficiency of the animal source food production model and its impact on the environment.

**What about health? Is not meat an essential food for our organism?**

This last question constitutes the counter argumentation paradigm of vegetarian diet, followed by *"it is not such a big deal; it is a matter of preference"*.

Well, no. Meat is not something our organisms needs and neither is it a grade of choice, when we see the numbers for health expenditure for meat consumption related diseases, especially in countries where health systems are public or mixed.

It is estimated that there is nearly 1.4 billions

people overweighed or suffering from obesity in the world [WHO, 2013a]. In Argentina, according to data gathered in 2009, 53,4% of the population presented some sort of weight excess and obesity increased significantly since 2005, from 14,6% to 18%. The province of Córdoba constitutes one of the country's regions in wich obesity prevails the most [Ferrate et al, 2009; Ferrante & Virgolini, 2007]: 35,4% of adult population has overweight and 18% is obese [MinSN, 2006], while 20-30% of children at elementary school suffer from obesity or are overweighed, depending on their age [SCP, 2010].

Due to its high and growing prevail, obesity is a serious public health issue in Argentina and in the rest of the world. [Wyatt et al, 2006; Ferrante et al, 2011]. Obesity is related to a great number of pathologies, such as type II diabetes, cardiovascular, cerebrovascular and locomotor system diseases, hepatic pathologies, infertility, and other diseases. A systematic review and meta-analysis recently published found a significant relation between obesity and all causes of death [Flegal et al, 2013]. Another review recently associated obesity as the major risk factor for cancer [De Pergola & Silvestris, 2013]. Besides, increasing evidence indicates that overweight and obesity during childhood and adolescence have adverse consequences on premature mortality and physic morbidity in adulthood [Reilly & Kelly, 2011].

Although obesity is a complex metabolic condition whose production mechanisms are not yet very clear, and in which even epigenetic phenomena can play a role during pregnancy, that is alterations in gene's expressions due to environmental influences [Martinez *et al*, 2012], other authors say that the key is in alimentary patterns [Bradley, 2012].

Many studies have examined the influence in dietary patterns on obesity, some of them analyzed the role meat products consumption plays in the risk of having obesity or on weight increase, and significant relations have been found. These associations can probably be made because meat consumption is associated to a greater intake of total fat, saturated fat, total calories and a cut in vegetables intake [Fung *et al*, 2004; Rosell *et al*, 2006; Vang *et al*, 2008; Wang & Beydoun, 2009].

Besides, many studies found a positive association between meat consumption (especially high consumption) and the risk of suffering from chronic and metabolic diseases, such as cardiovascular disease, type 2 diabetes and some types of cancer [Genkinger & Koushik, 2007; Vang *et al*, 2008; Sinha *et al* 2009; Micha *et al*, 2012; Pan *et al*, 2012, Rohrmann *et al*, 2013]. To the before mentioned, we should add current alimentary patterns, which have a great percentage of highly processed food based on corn and rich in sugar [García *et al*, 2012; Fletcher *et al*, 2013].

As I mentioned in previous chapters, the increase in meat consumption is a relatively recent phenomena dating halfway through the 21th century. Nevertheless, impacts in health and lifestyle population are important.

## 4.2 Diets Are Cultural

Before going on, let's consider a situation: the way in which we feed is plainly cultural.

The concept of culture is very broad and includes many things besides race and ethnic origins, as it also covers language, communication styles, social values and even religious behaviour. Food is part of it, and it is a reflection of geography, weather, and history of a given culture; this is why alimentary patterns have always depended on food availability in the region we reside and social customs.

These patterns remained more or less constant through time thanks to family and social knowledge transmission in successive generations. People in charge of children upbringing were (and are) responsible of instilling these alimentary patterns. This way we can objectivise that we never were sovereign upon our ways of feeding.

This exercise gets easier when we consider that the first foods we take after breastfeeding were those give by our carers (mother, father, uncles, grandparents, guardians), either because of customs or by a health professional's recommendation [Story et al, 2008].

In this way, the feeding habit becomes an unquestionable tradition because it constitutes a practice we carry out since some many years and to which there are not enough motives to question.

For example, in Argentina, roast is a very well known food and much wanted by great parts of society, it is closely related to social and family values. It consists in the cooking of different parts of the cow over embers, although it can also be calf meat, lamb and goat meat [VíaRestó, 2010]. If this roast is not eaten at commercial stores, it almost always implies an act of social encounter. Less abundant roasts are mainly Sunday best a family can have; nevertheless, big roasts which gather lots of people stand out (mainly families and friends). In this case, roast has many characteristics, almost ritualistic: at a big roast, only the cook or cooks intervene in the handling of the cooking, and when the meat is ready to be eaten guests usually use the phrase *"¡un aplauso para el asador!"* (*"A big hand for the cook!"*) [Fontoira, 2013].

The argentines identification with this typical food is such that a few years ago the Secretary of Culture of Argentina carried out a project to state that roast and other typically consumed in Argentina be considered Cultural, Alimentary and Gastronomic Heritage [Terra, 2003].

If we analyze the rest of the culture and contemplate the fact that being born in a given place as a random event, we can comprehend that if we had been born in México we would surely prefer spicy food, being corn and beans the pillars of our diet [Vargas & Montaño, 2010]. On the other hand, if we had been born in Japan, rice and fish would dominate in our diets [Demtriou, 2013]. We could go on this way with all world cultures.

As you can see, mainly, our diet depends on our environment, that is, the type of food available and our social habits. Investigators are also people and it is evident that the scientific community was never (nor is it) exempt of this dietary education.

## 4.3 Cultural Bias in Investigation

Groups of people that paid for these investigations were formed mainly by non vegetarians. This way, the majority of scientists investigating the issue (vegetarianism) probably did not notice or beat this cultural bias against meatless diets, bringing a growing concern over the potential dangers of vegetarian diets.

During the 60's there was a tendency to consider that population that lead a vegetarian diet had more risks of developing nutritional deficiencies that people who followed a meat based diet, weather it was because of the low protein or energy intake, or the lack of oligoelements (minerals). Although reports on nutritional deficiencies were based on particular cases or reports of children with compromised physical growth [Hardinge & Crooks, 1963; MacLean & Graham, 1980]. Because of this, to reduce the risk of lack of nutrients in meatless diets it was recommended to add a large amount of animal source foods such as eggs and dairy products [Register & Sonnenbeg, 1973].

A review of articles on vegetarian nutrition published from 1966 until 1995, by Sabate and colleagues, found that half of them dealt with deficiency diseases, nutritional status and growth [Sabate *et al*; 1999].

Numerous historical, methodological and sociological factors explain this emphasis on early biomedical literature on health risks related to vegetarian diets. From a historical perspective, it is not surprising that a few decades ago, the main focus of research on these diets were in nutritional status, as nutritional deficiency diseases were more prevalent in industrialized countries than today. Most of the early research on vegetarian nutrition were conducted on the health effects of short-term diet and cases of vegetarians who came to the clinic with health problems because it is much easier to prepare study cases that go to the community and identify vegetarians to follow in time and make a report on their health status, as required from the perspective of public health.

To this we can add a cultural aspect that greatly influenced these approaches: a cultural bias against meatless diets contributed to the growing concern about the potential risks of vegetarian diets. Until the '70s, those following vegetarian diets were assumed as anti-establishment, members of an underground culture or a religious sect [Dwyer *et al*, 1973].

The first serious scientific researches that contributed with favourable results for the adoption of a vegetarian diet were performed by Prof. Dr. Mervyn Hardinge during his doctoral dissertation at Harvard [Hardinge & Stare, 1954a; Hardinge & Stare, 1954b; Hardinge *et al*, 1962]. Over time, interest in this type of diet increased, and during the following years the results of nutritional epidemiological studies documented significant benefits of a vegetarian diet, such as reducing the risk of many chronic degenerative diseases and total mortality [Messina & Burke, 1997]. Although it did not yet ceases to be considered as riskier type of diet than those that included meat.

These new approaches were promoted because of the good health vegetarians showed in developed countries, which had low rates of obesity, heart disease, diabetes and many types of cancers, and increased longevity [Phillips *et al*, 1980; Snowdon *et al*, 1984; Snowdon & Phillips, 1985; Key & Davey, 1996]. This caused some curiosity in the researchers.

If there was a group that contributed significantly to these researches, it was the Seventh Day Adventists. For example, in 1989 the Adventist Health Study, which was a prospective cohort study on diet and health for more than 34000 people was published, they observed associations between chronic diseases and animal source food: protective factors were related to vegetal origin food and risk factors were related to animal origin food [Beeson *et al*, 1989].

The word "*paradigm*" has been used in science to refer to the theoretical framework and generally accepted view in a particular discipline at a given period of time. Thus, the paradigm refers to the assumptions, concepts, values and practices that constitutes a way of viewing reality.

In the book "The Structure of Scientific Revolutions", Thomas Kuhn coined the term "*paradigm shift*" to define sudden changes or advances in scientific thinking. A paradigm shift occurs when a "*conceptual world view is replaced by another*" [Kuhn, 1962].

Epidemiological, clinical and basic science research on the health effects of various plant foods is greatly expanding the understanding of the role of food in human health and nutrition. These recent scientific advances appear to have led to a paradigm shift: diets based on plant foods – such as well-balanced vegetarian diets – are now considered more as producers of improvement on human health than disease causing, in contrast to meat based diets.

## 4.4 Vegetarianism in Current Science

The first scientific nutritional attitudes towards vegetarianism were given by the American Dietetic Association (ADA), now called the Academy of Nutrition and Dietetics (AND). This institution has nearly 100 years and is one of the biggest nutrition and dietetics organization in the world, with about 72 thousand members. One of these positions was published in 1993 [Havala & Dwyer, 1993], which says:

> "It is the position of The American Dietetic Association that vegetarian diets are healthful and nutritionally adequate when appropriately planned."

Over time, the ADA made updated it and the last was published in 2009 [Craig & Mangels, 2009], stating that:

> "It is the position of the American Dietetic Association that appropriately planned vegetarian diets, including total vegetarian or vegan diets, are healthful, nutritionally adequate, and may provide health benefits in the prevention and treatment of certain diseases. Well-planned vegetarian diets are appropriate for individuals during all stages of the life

*cycle, including pregnancy, lactation, infancy, childhood, and adolescence, and for athletes."*

The transition from one position to another is rather clear, possibly influenced by the progress made by research in the lapse of time separating the two.

In addition to the reviews given by the Academy of Nutrition and Dietetics, there are other important institutions of nutrition and health who have declared their official stance on vegetarianism, among which we can find:

The Dietitians of Canada organization shares the position with the DNA and its official web site you can find article recommendations for vegetarians [Dietitians of Canada, 2013]. The Spanish Association of Dietitians-Nutritionists (AEDN) has opted for the same; you can find a Spanish translation of the position of the DNA in its official website [AEDN, 2009].

In August 2011, the British Dietetic Association (The British Dietetic Association BDA) published a fact sheet (Food Factsheet) on vegetarian food, written by nutritionist Lynne Garton [Garton, 2011]. It reads as follows:

*"Well-planned vegetarian diets can be healthy and nutritious. These have been associated with a lower risk of heart disease, type 2 diabetes, obesity, some cancers and reducing blood cholesterol levels.*

*[...] Well-planned vegetarian diets are appropriate for all stages of life."*

The Department of Agriculture and Health and Human Services of the United States published on 31 January 2011, the seventh edition of "Dietary Guidelines for Americans, 2010", an evidence-based nutritional guide that has a detailed section for a balanced vegetarian diet strictly adapted to nutritional needs, and highlights the benefits of the vegan diet to promote health, reduce the risk of chronic diseases and reduce prevalence of overweight and obesity. In this version of the guide, more attention is placed on vegetarian diets, devoting two full pages strictly to vegetarian nutrition [U.S. Department of Agriculture & U.S. Department of Health and Human Services, 2010].

In an article on vegetarianism on the website of the American Cancer Society we can read [ACS, 2010]:

> *"Some studies have linked vegetarian diets to lower risk for heart disease, diabetes, high blood pressure, obesity, and certain types of cancer, such as colon cancer. A strictly vegetarian diet must be properly planned to be sure it provides all the required nutrients."*

The Canadian Paediatric Society stated its official position in the Journal of Paediatric and Child Health in June 2010 [Amit, 2010]:

> *"Well-planned vegetarian and vegan diets with appropriate attention to specific nutrient components can provide a healthy alternative lifestyle at all stages of fetal, infant, child and adolescent growth."*

The American Academy of Paediatrics has an article on vegetarianism in children with recommendations thereon [AAP, 2013].

These are the official positions of the most important health institutions in the world. The rest tends to base its judgment on any of the above. We could say that global scientific consensus is that vegetarian diets meet all the nutritional needs at any stage of the life of a human being and can be practiced without fear of suffering from a nutritional deficiency.

## 4.5 Frequent Questioning

Although scientific evidence supports vegetarian diets, there are certain questions by the general public and some health professionals, who reject the idea that a vegetarian diet can be as or healthier than a diet that includes meat products. This idea is probably based on cognitive biases and lack of information.

However, some of them are real concerns about undervalued by vegetarians.

### 4.5.1 "Where do you get protein from if you do not eat meat?"

Proteins are large molecules that have the function of tissue growth and maintenance, and also are required for the formation of hormones and other physiological substances. But in reality, the technical term we use is the amino acid requirements, which are the molecules that make up proteins, like bricks that make up a wall. There are 20 amino acids, of which 9 humans can not synthesize and must be incorporated in our diets; these are called essential aminoacids [NIH, 2013a].

Those proteins having all the essential amino acids are called "complete" and those who do not possess all the essential amino acids are called "incomplete". Meat, eggs and dairy have complete proteins, while most plant products have incomplete proteins.

It was believed that it was necessary to consume all the amino acids at the same time to get the "complete protein", either by consuming foods with all amino acids or amino acids combining different foods at one meal, such as wheat (low in lysine) and beans (rich in lysine).

We now know that the body stores amino acids needed and used when needed, forming the so-called *pool* of amino acids, something like storage tanks, requiring only to incorporate different plant sources of amino acids throughout the day and even the week [Craig & Mangels, 2009].

In 1994, Young and Pellet wrote a review about it, collapsing the myths associated with vegetable proteins and their role in human nutrition [Young & Pellet, 1994]. It is mentioned that mixtures of plant proteins can serve as a complete and balanced source of amino acids to meet the metabolic needs.

A little more recent meta-analysis evaluated all studies on nitrogen balance and found no difference in the need for protein between different types of diets [Rand *et al*, 2003].

Therefore, plant foods based diets easily provide all

essential amounts of recommended amino acids for normal growth and development of human beings, and the combination of protein at each meal is unnecessary. Such is the case, some researchers are considering the importance of biotechnology and plant protein to meet the nutritional needs of future generations and avoid the environmental impact meat production entails [Day, 2013]. Some foods high in protein are:

- Grains: whole wheat flour, oats, barley, millet, brown rice.
- Legumes: chickpeas, lentils, beans, soybean, peas.
- Nuts: walnuts, hazelnuts, almonds.
- Seeds: sunflower, sesame, pumpkin.

### 4.5.2 "What about iron? Iron is in meat..."

Iron is an important mineral that serves multiple metabolic functions, from transporting oxygen and formation of haemoglobin in red blood cells, to participation in the metabolic processes of several enzymes. The body has about 3 to 4 grams of iron that cares very efficiently [NIH, 2013b].

There are two types of iron in food: heme iron found only in animal foods such as beef, chicken and fish; and non-heme iron is also found in animal foods and vegetables such as legumes, whole grains, nuts, seeds, green leafy vegetables and dried fruits.

However, non-heme iron is less well absorbed, but its absorption is significantly increased in the presence of vitamin C [Hallberg, 1981]. This led to think that vegetarians were more prone to iron deficiency anaemia than non-vegetarians and their ability to obtain iron from the diet was lower. However, iron deficiency is no more common in people who follow a vegetarian diet [Haddad *et al*, 1999] and these often incorporate much more of the mineral than people who follow a mixed diet through integral cereals [Davey *et al*, 2003].

Polyphenols such as tannins (coffee and tea) and phytates (legumes and cereals) may inhibit iron absorption, but the effect of various enhancers or inhibitors may be less important when the diet is varied, because factors are not in sufficient quantities to produce a significant effect on the overall absorption of iron [Reddy, 2005].

Humans successfully adapt to a wide range of requirements and intakes of iron [Cook, 1996], since absorption is regulated by the physiological demands and iron found in both the blood and in the reserves, is modified according to its bioavailability. For example, low levels of iron in the body cause increased intestinal absorption and decreased losses [Hunt & Roughead, 2000]. During pregnancy, women gain up to 60% the rate of iron absorption [Barret *et al*, 1994; Whittaker *et al*, 2001].

You should not worry about iron if the vegetarian diet is balanced, but if you are concerned that your iron intake may be poor, you could include foods that contain vitamin C to help absorption, like lemon.

### 4.5.3 Essential Fatty Acids

There are 2 types of essential fatty acids: omega-6 (linoleic) and omega 3 (alpha-linolenic). They are called so because they cannot be synthesized by the body and are

123

calculated fundamental molecules for complete nutrition in many animals, including humans, so they must be incorporated through food. Vegetarian diets are generally rich in omega 6 fatty acids, but may contain insufficient amounts of omega 3 fatty acids, being these very important for health.

Omega 3 fatty acids play an important role in health, particularly neurological and eye development, cardiovascular health and diseases with an inflammatory component [Yashodora *et al*, 2009]. According to their chemical characteristics, we can find 6 types of fatty acids, of which the most important are: alpha-linolenic acid (ALA), eicosapentaenoic acid (EPA) and docosahexaenoic acid (DHA). The first is abundant in plant sources (flax, chia), while the latter are abundant in animal sources such as fish [Siriwardhana *et al*, 2012]. Technically the EPA and DHA are not essential because the body can synthesize from the ALA, but as these are very important for neurological development and that there is some evidence that the conversion rate is relatively low, it was thought that vegetarians did not get enough EPA and DHA, transforming the consumption of omega 3 fatty acids in another headache for vegetarians [Craig & Mangels, 2009].

However, a recent study showed that although the intake of omega 3 fatty acids was lower in vegetarians, differences in blood were not significant, which could be explained by an adaptation of the organism that determines an increase in the conversion of ALA to EPA and DHA in vegetarians [Welch *et al*, 2010]. This supports the evidence that while DHA concentrations in breast milk and tissues are lower in vegetarians than non-vegetarians, there are no clear clinical differences between the two groups; therefore, the omega 3 needs of people who follow a vegetarian diet can be satisfied by the intake of dietary ALA [Sanders, 2009].

Despite this, vegetarians are not immunized against the deficit of EPA and DHA, so vegetarians should include good sources of ALA in their diet, such as flaxseed, walnuts, canola oil and soybean. People with higher requirements of omega-3 (pregnant and lactating) fatty acids, can benefit from DHA-rich microalgae.

### 4.5.4 B12 Vitamin

Vitamin B12 deficiency is not a myth and is a very important issue to address, as this vitamin deficiency is a common occurrence in the vegetarian population, especially among vegans (those who do not eat dairy or eggs) because this substance is found only in animal products [Pawlak *et al*, 2013; Obersby *et al*, 2013]. So much so, that there may be a deficiency of vitamin B12 in up to 50% of vegans [Glising *et al*, 2010]. A systematic review recently published in the Journal of European Clinical Nutrition, analyzed 40 well-designed studies about vitamin B12 deficiency in vegetarians and found that deficiency is around 45% in infants, 33% in adolescents, 39% in pregnant women and 89% in adults, being more common in strict vegetarians (vegans) than in lacto-ovo vegetarian [Pawlaw *et al*, 2014].

Vitamin B12, or cyanocobalamin, is a B vitamin that plays an important role in the body; it is involved in the formation of red blood cells and the maintenance of the central nervous system. Intake deficiency can manifest in a syndrome called pernicious anaemia, which can cause chronic persistent neurological symptoms such as confusion, depression and numbness in hands and feet [Aslinia et al, 2006]. However, it is very common to find vegetarians claiming to feel healthy despite not taking precautions regarding the intake of vitamin B12, which may be because vegetarian diets are typically rich in folic acid, which can mask the haematological symptoms of vitamin B12 deficiency and may go unnoticed until they manifest neurological symptoms [Herrmann et al, 2001].

There are foods that are presented as reliable sources of vitamin B12, such as fungi or spirulina. These foods contain an inactive form of B12 vitamin called pseudo vitamin B12; it interferes with the normal absorption of the active form [Watanabe, 2007]. Nonenriched vegetable origin foods do not have significant amounts of vitamin B12; and let's make it clear: Spirulina is not a good source of it [Watanabe et al, 2002].

There are groups of people who believe that the human body, or that the bacteria found in it, are able to synthesize enough vitamin B12 to meet the metabolic demands. This fact would be supported by a study conducted in 1980 by Albert and colleagues, who mention that human feces contain considerable amounts of this substance (and its analogues) that cannot be used by humans for not having the habit of coprophagia (eating feces) [Albert et al, 1980]. They also explain that in the small bowel there is considerable microflora capable of producing cyanocobalamin and their analogues. However, recently Allen and Stabler decided to identify and quantify the levels of cyanocobalamin and cobalamin analogues in human feces (something that has not been done so far), and found that over 98% of cyanocobalamin contained in feces was an analogue [Allen & Stabler, 2008], which is not usable by humans.

In short, you can lead a completely healthy vegetarian diet if you take the necessary precautions. If your diet does not include animal products (milk and eggs), you should make sure to incorporate vitamin B12 fortified food or take vitamin supplements [Craig & Mangels, 2009].

## 4.6 Benefits of Vegetarianism on Health

Once we agree that vegetarianism is a totally viable diet from the nutritional point of view, which is supported by the available scientific evidence, we can move to the analysis of the benefits adopting this diet could bring in public health.

As a result of research conducted on the morbidities associated with meat consumption, many scientists have recommended a vegetarian diet to prevent some chronic diseases and even obesity. A study in 2009 found that people who followed a vegetarian diet had lower rates of a number of health problems, like obesity and overweight, cardiovascular disease, hypertension, type 2 diabetes, some cancers, gallstones, kidney stones, constipation and diverticular disease [Lagiou *et al*, 2009].

However, the association between meat consumption and certain diseases is not enough to promote the adoption of a vegetarian diet as a health panacea, as it may not be necessary to stop eating meat to get some benefits.

## 4.6.1 Vegetarianism as Health Promotion and Prevention

Preventive medicine is the medical specialty responsible for the prevention of disease and is based on a set of actions and medical advice rather than the diagnose and treatment of diseases already established. This applies both in specialty or hospital care and primary care. There are several aspects according to the evolution of the disease, and we can distinguish three types of prevention in medicine [Salleras, 1994; Hensrud, 2000]:

Primary prevention

Primary prevention is done by removing the factors that could cause injury before they take effect. The intervention takes place before the disease occurs and its main objective is to prevent or delay the onset of it.

- Main Idea: Elimination of the causes and risk factors.

- Goal: Reduce the incidence of preventable diseases.

- Application: During the pre pathogenic period (before the beginning of the stimulus-induced factors that cause disease).

In turn, the prevention can be divided into two areas:

**Promoting health**: Targeting people. It is the promotion and protection of health of the population through actions that affect individuals in a community. For example, anti-smoking campaigns to prevent lung cancer and other diseases associated with tobacco, promoting the adoption of low-fat diets and physical activity to prevent the development of cardiovascular diseases.

**Health Protection**: It is performed on the environment. It is the promotion of environmental care and maintenance of the ecosystem of which we are part. Such as: maintaining forest areas, protecting the oceans, controlling carbon dioxide emissions, etc. Health protection activities are not carried out by the health professional personnel, but rather by other professionals related to the thematic, such as engineers, technicians, biologists, etc.

Secondary Prevention:

Secondary prevention is identifying and applying treatments to diseases at very early stages. The action takes place at the beginning of the disease, its main aim is to prevent or delay its development.

- Main Idea: Early diagnosis and treatment of disease.
- Objective: To reduce the prevalence of the disease.
- Application: In the preclinical period (when symptoms and signs are not fully established, but they are present in the subclinical embryonic state that can be checked with diagnostic methods).

Tertiary Prevention:

Tertiary prevention is performed when the disease has already developed and we are trying to prevent it from worsening and causing complications. The action takes place in full disease, its main objective is to eliminate or reduce the consequences of its development.

- Main Idea: Reduce damage by treatment and rehabilitation of established disease.
  - Objective: To reduce the prevalence of the disease.
  - Application: In the clinical period (when symptoms and signs have been established).

Quaternary Prevention:

Some authors consider that there is a fourth way: quaternary prevention is the set of health activities that mitigate or avoid the consequences of unnecessary or excessive interventions in the health system [Gofrit *et al*, 2000].

- Main Idea: Avoid over diagnosis and overtreatment in patients.
- Goal: To reduce the incidence of iatrogenic (damage caused by medical intervention)
- Implementation: During all phases of medical care.

As you can see, there are different levels of care. But there is only one that is the most efficient in providing adequate health care to the population, efficiently distributing valuable resources, using time wisely and above all things, eliminating the base problem. Clearly, primary prevention is the best bet we can do.

Precisely, the thesis that I will try to hold is that the vegetarian diet is an excellent dietary option to recommend in preventive medicine.

*4.6.2 Obesity and Overweight*

Most research shows that vegetarians, particularly strict vegetarians, tend to be leaner than non-vegetarians.

The Prospective Investigation of Cancer and Nutrition (EPIC-Oxford) study compared weight change over 5 years of almost 22 thousand men and women with different types of diets [Rosell *et al*, 2006]. Weight gain was lower in the vegetarian group where strict and shifted to a diet with less amount of animal source food during the period of monitoring. In turn, a significant difference in body mass index (BMI) was reported when adjusted for age and type of diet being meat eaters the ones with a higher BMI ($24,41$ kg/m$^2$ in men; $23,52$ kg/m$^2$ in women), while vegans had the lowest levels within normal parameters (BMI $22,49$ kg/m$^2$ in men, $21,98$ kg/m$^2$ in women), finally fish eaters and ovo-lacto vegetarians had intermediate values [Spencer *et al*, 2003]. Similar results were reported in the Adventist Health Study [Tonstad *et al*, 2009].

Epidemiological studies indicate that vegetarian diets are associated with lower BMI and lower prevalence of obesity in children and adults. A meta-analysis of studies on vegetarian diets in adults reported a smaller difference in vegetarian weight: 7,6 kg for men and 3,3 kg for women resulting in a BMI of less than 2 points. Similarly, compared with nonvegetarians, vegetarian children are thinner and their BMI difference becomes greater during adolescence [Sabate & Wien, 2010].

Finally, in 2006, after reviewing data from 87 studies, Berkow and Barnard indicated that a vegetarian diet can be highly effective for weight loss. Their review suggests that weight loss in vegetarians does not depend on physical exercise and occurs at a rate of about 400 grams per week, because ingested foods have more calories that burn easily instead of being stored as fat [Berkow & Barnard, 2006]. Recently, Farmer and colleagues also suggested that vegetarian diets may be better for weight control and also noticed that vegetarians tend to be thinner than people who eat meat [Farmer *et al*, 2011].

There are a number of possible explanations for this association: a lower fat intake, increased fibre intake and lower energy density foods. Some foods, like whole grains and nuts are consumed more frequently among vegetarians and were independently associated with a lower risk of obesity [Gaesser, 2007; Mattes, 2008].

Faced with this evidence, it is reasonable to adopt and promote a vegetarian diet for the prevention of obesity and overweight in children and adults.

### 4.6.3 Hypertension

Available evidence suggests that a vegetarian diet can help both the prevention and the management of arterial hypertension [Berkow & Barnard, 2005].

The EPIC-Oxford study found that people who ate no meat had lower prevalence of hypertension and lower systolic and diastolic blood pressure compared to those who ate meat; although this could be explained largely by differences in body mass index [Appleby *et al*, 2002]. The same thing happened recently in the 2nd Adventist Health Study [Petterson *et al*, 2012]. Variations in caloric intake and lifestyle of vegetarians may limit the strength of conclusions regarding the relationship between vegetarian diets and blood pressure.

However, few randomized clinical trials have shown that adopting a vegetarian diet can reduce blood pressure in normotensive and hypertensive individuals [Rouse *et al*, 1983; Margetts *et al*, 1986].

Although it is well accepted that both weight loss and reducing the intake of sodium (salt) can lower blood pressure [Appel, 2009], the effect of a vegetarian diet on blood pressure appears to be independent of the latter, suggesting that some components of the diet would be responsible [Rouse *et al*, 1986; Berkow & Barnard, 2005]. These results are consistent with the results of the DASH study (Dietary Approaches to Stopping Hypertension), in which subjects lead a low fat diet, rich in fruits, vegetables and dairy products, they found that considerable levels of potassium, magnesium and calcium in the diet play an important role in reducing blood pressure levels [Appel *et al*, 1997].

### 4.6.4 Diabetes

Vegetarian diets offer significant benefits for the prevention and management of diabetes mellitus type 2. Several observational studies have demonstrated a lower prevalence of type 2 diabetes in vegetarians than in nonvegetarians [Snowdon & Phillips, 1985; Fung *et al*, 2004; Tonstad *et al*, 2009].

This finding has been well documented through the Adventist Health Study. In the original study of Adventist Health covering about 25 thousand people found that vegetarians had about half the risk of developing diabetes than nonvegetarians, as well as showing a significant association between red meat consumption and the risk of diabetes, regardless of weight and physical activity [Snowdon & Phillips, 1985]. More recently, in the 2nd Adventist Health Study covering about 60000 people, it was found that the prevalence of diabetes in vegetarians was almost 30% lower compared to non-vegetarians, meanwhile a positive correlation was found between meat consumption and risk of type 2 diabetes [Tonstad et al, 2009].

The reason for the lower prevalence of type 2 diabetes in vegetarians is not yet clear. Some authors suggest that increased consumption of plant foods such as whole grains, vegetables, fibre and nuts are protective factors [Craig & Mangels, 2009], while others attribute it to the lack of animal soruce foods, either by heme iron intake [Jiang et al, 2004; Luan et al, 2008] and by the intake of animal protein [Schulze et al, 2003; Fung et al, 2004].

A recently conducted meta-analysis and systematic review of 12 cohort studies suggests a positive association between meat consumption and type 2 diabetes. The authors suggested that the consumption of 120 grams/day of red meat increases by 20% the risk for diabetes and 50 grams/day of processed meat increases it by 57% [Aune et al, 2009].

However, some interventions have evaluated the effects of a vegetarian diet on diabetes, such as the one carried out by Barnard and colleagues, comparing the tracking of a low-fat vegetarian diet (49 people) with the tracking diet recommended by the American Diabetes Association (50 people). They found that the group that followed the vegetarian diet are more reduced glycosylated haemoglobin levels compared to the other group and nearly half reduced their medication [Barnard et al,

2006].

But as patients who followed a vegetarian diet had a greater decrease in weight, it is difficult to discern whether the improvements observed in diabetic patients who followed the vegetarian diet were due to weight reduction (improvement in blood glucose levels) or the diet itself, in addition to what was mentioned some lines above [Barnard *et al*, 2009].

*4.6.5 Cardiovascular Diseases*

The most consistent evidence to health benefits of a vegetarian diet is reducing the risk of coronary heart disease and deaths caused by it (ischemic heart disease). Numerous studies and authors have proven this fact several years ago and over time it has been confirmed [Phillips *et al*, 1978; Burr & Butland, 1988; Chang-Claude *et al*, 2005; AHA, 2013].

Two large cohort studies [Frasser, 1999; Appleby *et al*, 2002] and a meta-analysis [Key *et al*, 1999], found that vegetarians had a 30% lower risk of death due to ischemic heart disease than non-vegetarians. This lower risk of death was observed in both lacto-ovo vegetarians and strict vegetarians. The difference in risk persisted after BMI adjustment, smoking habits and social class, which is important because the lower BMI commonly seen in vegetarians is a factor that may help explain the lower risk of heart disease in vegetarians.

This was supported by a recent systematic review and meta-analysis by Huang and colleagues, which included a total of approximately 124 thousand people from around the world and concluded that vegetarians had significantly lower mortality from cardiovascular disease than non-vegetarians, exactly 29% less [Huang *et al*, 2012].

These results are logical if one considers that vegetarians generally have better lipid profile than non-vegetarians, with lower levels of total cholesterol and low density lipoprotein (LDL) [De Biase *et al*, 2007, Rao & Al-Weshahy, 2008], lower levels of triglycerides [Zhang *et al*, 2013], lower BMI and a lower incidence of diabetes and hypertension; all risk factors that contribute to the development of cardiovascular disease [NHS, 2012].

Given that cardiovascular and cerebrovascular diseases are the leading cause of death worldwide [WHO, 2013b], vegetarian diets should be taken into account when assessing the possibility of improving the overall health status and lower the costs of public health from these diseases. Anyway, the key to a successful vegetarian diet is to eat in a healthy way, as the type of diet per se, is not miraculous [Fraser, 2009].

### 4.6.6 Cancer

Some research suggests that vegetarians have a lower overall rate of cancer in the general population and life expectancy appears to be greater [Fraser, 2009, Key *et al*, 2009]. The Adventist Health Study showed that non-vegetarians had a significantly higher risk of colorectal and prostate cancer compared to vegetarians, but no significant differences in lung, breast, uterus or stomach cancer after adjusting for age, sex and smoking [Fraser, 1999].

Despite this, these epidemiological studies are inconclusive and more research is needed.

The cancer that does present evidence of having less impact on the vegetarian population is, without doubt, colorectal cancer. Probably the most crucial factor in this type of cancer is high fibre intake by vegetarians [Ben *et al*, 2013], lower BMI and abdominal fat [Hong *et al*, 2012]. The volume increase effect in faecal bulk that dietary fibre produce, can increase the carcinogenic substances transit speed by the intestine and reduce the exposure to mutagenic compounds in surface contact with the intestinal wall [Fardet, 2010]. Also, people who follow a vegetarian diet have a different colonic environment because they tend to have lower proliferation of cells in the colon, different bacterial profiles and lower levels of faecal mutagens [van Dokkum *et al*, 1983; O'Keefe, 2008; Schatzkin *et al*, 2008].

The benefits of vegetarian diets on cancer have been associated with protective compounds related to cancer prevention and stunting cancer cells. Foods that are pillars in vegetarian diets (whole grains, legumes, fruits and vegetables) are rich in fibre, folic acid, phytochemicals and antioxidants [Dewell *et al*, 2008]. Phytochemicals, including carotenoids, ascorbate, tocopherol, selenium, isothiocyanates, indoles, phenols, protease inhibitors, plant sterols and other biologically active compounds possess anticancer activity [Gullett *et al*, 2010; Liu, 2013; Vallinas Gonzalez *et al*, 2013]. However, more well-designed clinical trials are needed to confirm these findings [Priyadarsini & Nagini, 2012].

We have a good degree of certainty about one thing, that the meat has a high carcinogenic activity, especially when it is consumed in large quantities as demonstrated by the European Prospective Investigation into Cancer and Nutrition recently performed [Rohrmann *et al*, 2013]. This is because high fat and animal protein diets, and red meat cooked at high temperatures, may increase the risk of developing cancer by releasing carcinogenic compounds [Cross *et al*, 2007; Sinha *et al*, 2009; Lam *et al*, 2009].

### 4.6.7 Other Diseases

Some research suggested that a vegetarian diet can reduce the risk of other health problems. Although these results are positive and add to the evidence of the benefits of a vegetarian diet, the small number of these requires confirmation by deeper and more systematic investigations. Some of these conditions are:

**Diverticular Disease:** Vegetarians tend to have a lower incidence of diverticular disease than non-vegetarians. Probably due to the high intake of dietary fibre by incorporating whole grains, vegetables, fruits, legumes and nuts [Nair & Mayberry, 1994; Humes & West, 2011]. Maybe some people suffering from diverticulosis or diverticulitis are surprised at this, but a vegetarian diet is apt to be carried out by people with these conditions because the consumption of foods with seeds and the risk of complications is simply a myth [Talerton & DiBaise, 2011].

**Gallstones:** In a cohort study with 800 women between 40 and 69 years old, non-vegetarians were more than twice likely to develop gallstones than vegetarian, even after controlling for BMI and age [Pixley *et al*, 1985]. Although a recent study found no significant relationship between vegetarian diets and the protective effect against gallstones [Walcher *et al*, 2010]. However, the low incidence of obesity and overweight in the vegetarian population and low intake of fat, which are risk factors for developing gallstones, support the idea that a vegetarian diet may have a protective factor against this disease.

**Gout:** Some research suggests that the gout could have lower incidence in vegetarians. A study of nearly 50 thousand older male individuals of 12 years compared the diets suffering with gout and found that not eating meat, especially red meat, significantly increased the risk of gout [Choi *et al*, 2004]. Another study examined the effect of different diets on the risk of crystallization of uric acid, he found it was higher in people with high levels of meat consumption is lower in people who ate a vegetarian diet [Siener & Hesse, 2003].

**Rheumatoid Arthritis:** Several studies have shown that people with rheumatoid arthritis may benefit by adopting a vegetarian diet. A systematic review of randomized controlled studies on groups recently found a clinically and statistically significant effect of vegetarian diets on this pathology [Smedslund *et al*, 2010]. The exact mechanism of these improvements is not clear, an analysis found that weight loss does not contribute significantly to the improvement so when individuals follow a vegetarian diet [Sköldstam *et al*, 2005], it

139

may be as a result of the anti-inflammatory effect produced by the diet [Elkan *et al*, 2010].

**Renal Disease:** A review found that high consumption of animal protein can have adverse effects on people with kidney disease and that replacing animal protein by vegetable protein produces a protective effect against the development of proteinuria (protein in urine) in patients with diabetes, as well as indicating that the vegetarian diet is adequate to meet the nutritional needs of patients with chronic kidney disease who often have deficiencies of this nutrient [Bernstein *et al*, 2007]. It can also help keep phosphorus homeostasis [Moe *et al*, 2011]. A study of individuals with type 2 diabetes and macroalbuminuria (too much protein in the urine), found that eliminating red meat from the diet and following a vegetarian diet low in protein, improved renal function and lipid profile [de Mello *et al*, 2006].

**Constipation:** Vegetarians tend to have lower incidence of constipation due to increased consumption of dietary fibre than nonvegetarians [Craig & Mangels, 2009].

**Cataracts:** People who follow a vegetarian diet seem to have a lower risk of cataracts than non-vegetarians, probably because of the increased consumption of fruits and vegetables [Appleby *et al*, 2011].

Finally, a study involving nearly a hundred thousand people found that vegetarian diets are associated with lower mortality from all causes and some reductions in cause-specific mortality

[Orlich *et al*, 2013].

We should not oversee this so I will quote a recent study by Burkert and colleagues which has spread among the web and the anti-vegetarian groups. This study, "Nutrition and Health - Association between eating behaviour and various health parameters: a study sample" [Burkert *et al*, 2014], concludes that *"Our study has shown that Austrian adults who consume a vegetarian diet are less healthy (in terms of cancer, allergies, and mental health disorders), have a lower quality of life, and also require more medical treatment"*. This research has spread everywhere due to sensationalist media and the limited capacity to analyse a scientific study by the general population. But the fact is that it represents a study with several limitations: it is cross-sectional cohort, this means that the groups were evaluated at a given moment and not for a long period as required by epidemiological studies. Another mistake is to have included fish eaters in the "vegetarian" group, and these accounted for more than half of the group: 185 out of 339. Therefore, the results provided by the study are unreliable.

As you can see, vegetarian diets, as well as being nutritionally adequate, they can provide health benefits to prevent and help manage certain diseases, so it should be taken seriously when planning public health and promoting a healthy diet.

# Some myths...

*Translation: María Agustina Graglia*

## 5.1 The myth of acid and alkaline diets

This is a myth that we must disassemble, not just because it is academically incorrect, but because many pseudoscientific applications that can endanger the life of many people derive from it. Perhaps many of you have already heard of it. It is about the belief that food can cause changes in the pH of the body and, according to the values of it, you can achieve perfect health or diseases such as cancer.

I am going to use an article published in the blog "Club Nutricional" in this regard, which content does not differ from what it is postulated by its advocates [Club Nutricional, 2011]. According to them, there are foods, called antiphysiological, that acidify the body. Some of them are: refined sugar, refined salt, all types of meat, bakery products, margarines, soft drinks, caffeine, alcohol, snuff, drugs, and any food that is cooked or that contains conservatives, colorants or flavorings. Besides, there are foods that alkalize the body, like raw vegetables, fruits, seeds, whole grains, honey, plants' chlorophyll, water, and even exercise.

This idea is based on a complete unawareness of the functioning of the human body and of the accepted mechanisms of the formation of cancer cells. The myth says that acidifying foods cause a harmful surrounding for normal cells, because a decrease of the pH causes the "expel of oxygen from the cells" and therefore, without it, they become cancer cells. This myth is usually spread jointly with another one that involves John Hopkins' Hospital of the United States, which authorities would have accepted the "evidence" of erroneous facts regarding cancer. However, the hospital has drafted an article on its website belying this fact [JHM, 2009].

### 5.1.1 Otto Heinrich Warburg

Apparently, it all started with a manipulation of the information provided by a scientist named Otto Heinrich Warburg, who was awarded with a Nobel Prize in Physiology or Medicine for his "Discovery of the nature and mode of action of the respiratory enzyme" [The Nobel Prize Foundation]. This labor meant a milestone in the biochemical comprehension of numerous organic processes, and it was considered by some as the most original and productive labor of the 20th century.

The respiratory enzyme is part of the oxidation chain that takes place in the mitochondria in order to obtain energy in the shape of ATP (adenosine triphosphate, the energy "currency" of the cell) from glucose and through a process called Krebs Cycle. For this process to occur oxygen is needed. This way of transforming glucose into energy using oxygen is called aerobic glycolysis.

Warburg was a great scientist, and the results of many of his research became pillars for organic chemistry and human physiology. But his research on cancer was less fruitful. From observing that cancer cells could reproduce without oxygen, he proposed the hypothesis that oxygen deprivation was the cause of the disease. According to this theory, body cells that "do not use" oxygen would develop cancer. Today, we know that there are normal cells that do not do it: red blood cells, cells from the cornea, the lens, and certain regions of the retina.

Warburg also detected that cancerous tissues grew in acid environments, that is, in environments which pH was lower than the body's (7.4) and that normal cells metabolize glucose differently to cancer cells. This research led him to write "The metabolism of tumors" (Stoffwechsel der Tumoren) [Warburg *et al*, 1924].

Afterwards, in 1956, he wrote an article that was published in the Science journal, titled "On the origin of cancer cells" [Warburg, 1965] where he gave signs of the consequences that it would trigger. Ten years later, he presented his work "The prime cause and prevention of cancer" in Germany's reunion of Noble Prices [Warburg, 1966].

The ideas proposed by Warburg were well received and permeated in the moment. According to him, many respiratory enzymes, vitamins from the B complex and iron were to be introduced in the diet. This would help prevent the emergence of cancer, and it would add on to treatments done through megadoses of vitamins, as proposed by Linus Pauling (awarded with a Nobel Prize in Chemistry and in Peace), who began orthomolecular "medicine". Nowadays this theory only has historical interest, and they are both pseudoscientific.

### 5.1.2 What actually happens

What Warburg proposed was a very interesting reasoning, if you take into account the developed knowledge until that time. But, what we currently know is that the absence of oxygen in tumor cells is due to their high growth rate: about 200 times higher than normal cells.

It is necessary to explain some technical processes to comprehend what happens in the body. To transform glucose into energy, the cell must perform a series of well-defined steps, whereby if one component is missing, everything fails. Initially, glucose is transformed into a substance called pyruvic acid or pyruvate, which can follow two paths:

1. When there is oxygen: aerobic glycolysis is performed. This happens in the vast majority of our cells, with some exceptions (like I mentioned above). Pyruvate enters the mitochondria to undergo oxidative phosphorylation (in which the enzymes that Warburg discovered participate) producing energy.

2. When there is no oxygen: a stage of hypoxia is produced and anaerobic glycolysis is performed. Pyruvate cannot enter the mitochondria, it is transformed into lactic acid or lactate and then converted into energy.

The first path produces a lot of energy, whereas the second one does not. But **this does not make one better than the other**; they are simply fantastic mechanisms of adaptation to different metabolic stages. For instance, when we perform an intense physical activity (a 100-meters sprint or escaping from a hunter in a distant past), the oxygen demand to produce energy increases so much that sometimes it cannot be satisfied, for what the cell must avail itself of the energy provided by anaerobic glycolysis, however small it might be. This situation causes the concentration of lactate in the cell to be increased and to be expelled outwards (it is that compound what produces a feeling of "burning" in the muscles).

Exactly the same happens in tumors: cancer cells have such a high metabolism that they need great amounts of oxygen to function. When not able to satisfy that demand, they perform anaerobic glycolysis to obtain energy. This is known as Warburg Effect, and it leads to a huge production of lactic acid and to the creation of an acidic microenvironment [Gatenby & Gillies, 2004]. As we can see, this acidification is not a result of a diet, but of the metabolism of cancer. Besides, **acidification or alkalization never happen in our body** (in normal situations), because the pH is jealously kept in a very narrow range, between 7.35 and 7.45, and exceeding it either way can result in death.

As a curiosity, a hypothesis on the origin of cancer has recently been elaborated based on the Warburg Effect. According to it, an alteration in the route of energy production would produce reactive forms of oxygen to accumulate, which would cause, at the same time, damage in the genetic material

147

of the cell, and it would end in the production of cancer [Kim & Dang, 2006]. But this is only a hypothesis and needs further development.

### 5.1.3 Foods are important, but they do not acidify the body

In my opinion, when following a diet, it is necessary not to take as a parameter whether foods are or not acid or alkaline. The inside of the stomach is so acid that no food can change its acidity. Only when food enters the duodenum, pancreatic and liver secretions neutralize the stomach acids making the food alkaline. The modification of the diet cannot change the acidity of any body part, except from urine, which does not have repercussions in health.

Promoters of this myth say that cancer cells cannot live in an alkaline environment, which is true, but no other body cell can. Unfortunately, we still know very little about cancer, although great strides have been made. We know that cancer is not a single disease nor it has a single cause, but it is a group of multi-causal diseases, for what it is more difficult to study. Many things in our genes, our life style and the environment that surrounds us can increase or decrease the risk of suffering from cancer. This way and at this moment, we can take preventive measures in this regard and decrease the probability of getting it.

The report "Food, Nutrition, Physical Activity, and the Prevention of Cancer" published by the World Cancer Research Fund and the American Institute for Cancer Research [WCRF/AICR, 2007] recommends:

• Stay as lean as possible, within the normal weight range.

• Do between 30 and 60 minutes of moderate physical activity daily. For instance, walking.

• Avoid sweetened drinks and junk food.

• If you are a mother, breastfeed for at least 6 months.

• Do not eat more than half a kilo of red meat per week and avoid processed meat.

• Limit the intake of alcoholic drinks to one daily measure for women, and two for man.

• Eat 5 daily servings of fruit and vegetables.

• Limit the consumption of salt to 6 daily grams; avoid its intake as a preservative.

• Avoid dietary supplements, except for folic acid during pregnancy.

• If you survive cancer, follow nutritional recommendations from a professional, do physical activity, and maintain an adequate weight.

## 5.2 Acid Diets, Milk and Osteoporosis

Another fairly spread myth (directly related with the mentioned above) is the one that relates the consumption of dairy products with the acidity of the body. It states that proteins and phosphates from milk, and dairy products in general, produce acids that cause body acidification and the so-called modern diseases, osteoporosis among them.

To begin with, there is no scientific evidence that

supports these ideas: nor milk or dairy are acid producers, nor our body acidifies because of our diet. Besides, there is also no evidence that supports a relationship between dairy consumption and modern diseases.

In relation to this, we can find statements like the following:

> "Milk and dairy products are not healthy because they produce calcium loss through urine and accelerate calcium deception from bones. It has been demonstrated that countries that consume more quantity of dairy products, animal protein and calcium have high rates of osteoporosis and hip fracture."

According to a food classifying system much quoted by those who defend this theory [Remer & Friedrich, 1995], milk is defined as a slightly acid product, based on the idea that it has ionic phosphates and sulfates, which are acid. A portion of these are excreted through urine. This way, it seems like the consumption of milk and proteins (what would be an acid diet) leads to the excretion of acids and to the deterioration of bone health. This supposed damage of bone health would be due to the observation that a greater acid excretion through urine is associated with a greater concentration of calcium in it, thus, bones decalcify.

### 5.2.1 What does available evidence say?

Firstly, there is no scientific evidence that supports the

idea of phosphate and sulfate intake from milk being harmful for bone health, because even though the amount of calcium excreted through urine increases with the amount of acid excreted, it is more important that the balance of calcium itself remains unmodified.

A multidisciplinary team of scientists from the University of Calgary conducted a systematic review and meta-analysis of studies that analyzed how diet and supplements could alter the excretion of acids or alkalis, and how diet altered calcium balance and calcium excretion through urine [Fenton *et al*, 2009]. This paper showed that, indeed, a greater urinary acid excretion, when consuming a diet high in protein, was associated with a greater urinary calcium excretion. However, when calcium balance was examined, no association was found between calcium excretion and calcium balance. Therefore, evidence does not support the statement "foods that cause acid excretions are harmful for calcium balance" despite this mineral's presence in the urine.

Secondly, dairy products do not produce acid in the body. One study on urinary acid excretion after milk intake demonstrated that milk makes urine more alkaline than cola drinks and water [Heaney & Rafferty, 2001]. The most interesting thing about this study is that the water that was used was distilled, which means it could provide neither acids nor alkalis, unlike cola drinks, which provided phosphoric acid, causing a greater urinary acid concentration. Meanwhile, another study compared acid net excretions caused by regular milk with those caused by soy milk and found that there was no difference between them [Spence *et al*, 2005].

## 5.2.2 Milk does not produce osteoporosis

The statement *"fracture rate due to osteoporosis is higher in countries that consume more dairy products, calcium and animal protein"* implies a comparison among cultures. Assuming that fracture rates are different because diets are different is a rather poor and slanted conclusion. Other important risk factors are involved in the development of osteoporosis and hip fracture. These factors are not related with what different cultures consume, but with genetic differences, physical activity, exposure to sunlight (which allows vitamin D synthesis), among others [Mayo Clinic, 2013]. A variation in any of these factors can explain the different fracture rates in different cultures. Thereby, it is not right to assume that dairy causes these pathologies without previously taking into account every conditioning factor mentioned above.

The best available evidence supports that the most important risk factors in osteoporosis and hip fracture are: sedentarism [Nikander *et al*, 2010] and poor calcium intake throughout life [Tang *et al*, 2007]. In fact, a person that lives in a big city in Asia, where physical activity is perhaps similar to that of western cultures, has almost identical hip fracture rates to that of industrialized countries.

Even though observations function as triggers to ask yourself questions and conduct studies, it is not correct to assume the causes of a phenomenon based solely on observations, especially when these are associated with a fact with so many possible variables.

This mistake can be summarized in the phrase

**"Correlation does not imply causation"**. In order to know if phenomenon A produces phenomenon B, there not only has to be a statistical relationship between them, but there must be a mechanism of action for A to produce B. Clearly this is not the case.

Finally, a systematic review and meta-analysis recently conducted on the theory that acid diets produce bone disease, concludes that: "Causal association between acidic diet and osteoporosis is not supported by evidence and there is no evidence that an alkaline diet is protective of bone health" [Fenton *et al*, 2011].

*5.2.3 Milk is not the best source of calcium*

However, I will add that according to a report recently released by Harvard School of Public Health, calcium is important (as it is well known) but **milk is not the best source of this mineral**, since a large amount of milk intake is associated with prostate cancer and ovarian cancer. Besides, it is high in saturated fats and contains hormones that might be harmful to health [HSPHa].

This was reinforced in its last publications "Healthy Eating Plate" and "Healthy Eating Pyramid" where the following is mentioned: *"The guidelines' recommendation to increase the intake of low-fat milk and dairy products seems to reflect the interests of the powerful dairy industry more so than the latest science. There is little, if any, evidence that eating dairy prevents osteoporosis or fractures, and there is considerable evidence that high dairy product consumption is*

153

*associated with increased risk of fatal prostate and maybe ovarian cancers."* [HSPHb].

In conclusion, high quality scientific evidence reveals that milk and dairy products do not cause body acidification. On the other hand, dairy products do not produce acid in our metabolism, and our bodies do not acidify because of our modern diet. Besides, scientific evidence does not support associations between a large amount of milk and dairy products intake and the development of osteoporosis, when taking into account other important factors such as physical activity.

## 5.3 We are not vegetarians by nature

This is perhaps one of the most widespread myths among vegetarians. Generally, you can find articles on the Internet showing tables that compare the anatomy and physiology of carnivores and herbivores animals with those of human beings. These tables compare features such as the shape of teeth, the acidity of gastric juice, the presence of certain enzymes, the length of the gut, and the characteristics of the feces. They conclude that human beings must be vegetarian or fruitarian to follow their nature, because they are more "similar" to herbivores than to carnivores.

### 5.3.1 Error from logic

To begin with, this argument uses a fallacy called "Naturalistic Fallacy" which takes places every time someone identifies "natural" with "good" or "better" [Moore, 1903].

Therefore, the statement *"we are vegetarians by nature"* falls into this error, since there is an attempt to demonstrate that being vegetarian is right because it is natural.

It would be like affirming that women must devour their husbands after their first intercourse, because that is what some spiders do in the natural world. Or that cobra venom is healthy because it comes from nature, as well as mercury, cyanide or arsenic.

## 5.3.2 Error from science

The statement is not only a fallacy, but it is also academically incorrect. Actually, we are opportunistic omnivores, capable of consuming both animal and plant products.

Much of the erroneous information on this subject comes from the existing confusion around the taxonomic and dietetic characteristics of living beings. Dietary adaptations are not limited to the simple dichotomy of herbivores (strict vegetarians) and carnivores (strict meat-eaters). Frugivorous (who eat mostly fruit), grainivores (who eat mostly nuts and seeds), folivorous (who are leaf-eaters), insectivores (who eat insects and small vertebrates), among others, must be taken into account. It is also important to remember that morphology (anatomy or physiology) and functioning (behavior) do not always have a one on one relationship. Individual anatomic structures can serve one or more functions and similar functions can be performed in many different ways [McArdle, 1991]. Let us remember that biological evolution is not perfect. Wisdom teeth are a sign of that.

### 5.3.3 We are omnivores

Our species (Homo sapiens) has a very varied diet, reflection of biological and behavioral acquisitions from our most distant ancestors. Much of our adaptive success can be attributed to the metabolic and physiological changes that evolution shaped; but also, to our abilities for sourcing, preparing and consuming of food. It all allowed humans to adapt to environmental changes that happened in the Planet throughout more than four million years. Our biological history model, our brain expansion, some dental modifications, and even technological and cultural evolution are, partly, a result of dietary changes throughout evolution.

Omnivores are defined as generalized feeders, with neither carnivore nor herbivore specialization to acquire or process food, and they are capable of consuming both animal and plant protein. They are basically opportunistic feeders (they survive with what is available) with more generalized anatomic and physiological characteristics, especially in relation to teeth [National Geographic; McArdle, 1991].

### 5.3.4 The evolution of our diet: Australopithecus and Paranthropus

The species of Australopithecus (A. anamensis, A. afarensis, A. africanus, A. bahrelghazali, A. garhi, A. sediba) are a diverse and numerous group. With its great diversity in Eastern and Southern Africa, Australopithecus consumed leaves and fruits on regular basis, but also tubercles, roots, invertebrates, and small vertebrates. Basically, we can compare their diet to the soft and rich in carbohydrates diet that chimpanzees and gorillas have today [Henry *et al*, 2012; Wynn *et al*, 2013]. Australopithecus frequented riparian forests and forested surroundings as well as more open areas, and adapted their diet to the available resources in each area, like it currently happens with chimpanzees, gorillas and baboons [Estebaranz *et al*, 2012]. However, studies of carbon isotopes obtained from their bone remains indicate that they commonly consumed vegetables and juicy fruits. Some evidence also suggests that at least some of these species could have eaten meat. The shape and microwear of teeth, as well as the functioning of the jaw and the structure of the skull (intended for chewing) attest it [Sponheimer *et al*, 1999].

About 2.6 million years ago the Earth's climate became colder and more arid [Tipple, 2013]. In Africa, part of the wood disappeared, giving way to open landscapes [Magill *et al*, 2013a]. These changes in the landscape drastically altered food resources that were offered to hominids by the surrounding. Plants that grow in semiarid regions, or where there is at least seasonal aridity, are very different from those that grow in a more humid environment, where Australopithecus used to live. Vegetation that spread throughout Eastern and Southern Africa made adaptations to save water and resist drought. Among the typical adaptations to aridity we find leathery leaves, wax covers of difficult digestion, thorns on the stems, and a lack of succulent fruits [Magill *et al*, 2013b].

In response to that environmental change, the Paranthropus species emerged, which was a very robust species, with a brain that was similar to the one of Australopithecus, and with an extraordinarily powerful chewing

157

apparatus. Their jaw was very high, large and robust, and it was associated to a powerful musculature. Cheekbones remarkably widened to allow very powerful temporary muscles to go behind them. These were inserted in the sagittal crest, which was very developed in some specimens. Their teeth also changed, the incisors were reduced and molars and premolars were widened, which enabled a large surface for grinding food [Rotman, 2005; Wood & Constantino, 2007].

These adaptations allowed Paranthropus to process the food that they could find in their surroundings. Dry fruits, seeds, fleshy rhizomes, and succulent roots from the vegetation that had adapted to aridity could be strongly mashed before swallowing, which facilitated subsequent digestion. On the other hand, their vegetarian lifestyle did not require a greater intellectual capacity than the one they already had, for what their brains were not under any evolutionary pressure to increase their size [Constantino, 2013].

### 5.3.5 Early Homo and meat consumption

Another group of hominids chose a very different solution from that of Paranthropus in adapting to the new environment that was spreading across Africa over two million years ago. While Paranthropus became specialists in eating hard vegetables, these other ones chose to become very efficient opportunists. One opportunistic strategy was based on taking advantage of any resource that was within reach. This required a versatile behavior and a capacity for improvisation, which were accomplished because of a greater intelligence.

This solution adopted by the species of the genus Homo,

caused a remarked increase of their brain size [Van Arsdale, 2013]. Early Homo had skulls with a greater encephalic volume than those of Australopithecus: Homo habilis reached a cranial capacity of about 700 cm³, with an average of about 600 cm³. However, having a greater brain has its drawbacks, as it requires a greater amount of food to satisfy the demand of energy that is needed to keep the brain active [Dorey, 2013].

Almost 10% of the energy that a chimpanzee requires to keep its metabolism at rest is consumed by brain cells (a similar percentage to that of Australopithecus and Paranthropus). However, for modern humans that number goes up to almost 25%. A single neuron from the brain cortex uses about 4.7 million ATP (adenosine triphosphate) per second [Zhu *et al*, 2012]. For Homo habilis, the brain consumed 15% of the required energy to keep the metabolism at rest [Shultz *et al*, 2012]. But, the dietary demands of a larger brain are not limited to the amount of energy, but the quality of the food is also fundamental for the development of the brain. For instance, the brain needs fatty acids for the nervous system to develop normally, which are especially found in dry fruits and animal fats. But in the Pleistocene, the only abundant and constant source of fatty acids was animals, apart from being an excellent source of energy [Crawford, 1990, Leonard *et al*, 2010].

Therefore, early Homo encountered a dilemma: his survival in the new more hostile environment relied on increasing the size of his brain to become more versatile in his behavior and take advantage of the available resources in each moment, but in return he had to find additional sources of energy.

Thus, these hominids changed their almost exclusively vegetarian diet for one that was higher in animal protein and animal fats. This way, they initiated the process of developing an increasingly complex intelligence that was unique among primates [Van Arsdale, 2013]. The increase of brain size demanded hominids to become omnivorous, but in order to obtain meat and fat they had to be even smarter.

This is how having a larger brain became an evolutionary advantage: hominids developed new behaviors and strategies for acquiring new food and taking advantage of it, such as the development of lithic technology (made from stones) through the creation of small sharp devices and tools to hit and break bones, all of which improved the access to meat from animal carcasses and to bone marrow [Shultz *et al*, 2012; Dorey, 2013].

### 5.3.6 Neanderthals

Neanderthals inhabited hostile regions in Central Europe, and also more benign climates in the Mediterranean and Middle East. To survive in such different environments, they had to adapt their diet to the resources available in each region [Fiorenza *et al*, 2011]. In cold regions meat was the basic resource (as shown by isotopic studies) [Richards *et al*, 2000], complemented with vegetables when available. On the other hand, in coastal regions of the Mediterranean, they exploited marine resources such as different invertebrates, turtles, etcetera [Henry *et al*, 2010].

Neanderthals had large brains, and their body size was

imposing and robust: their skeleton, muscles and tissues formed a human machine of great power. Without a doubt, they were efficient in searching for food and in their daily physical activities [Helmuth, 1998]. But, these very robust bodies had also important metabolic constraints. It has been estimated that maintaining and moving a body of that size would imply between 3000 and 5000 kcal/day for a Neanderthal woman, and between 4000 and 6000 kcal/day for a man. This would also imply a very high intake of nutrients to counteract the metabolic expense, which requires a very important caloric intake [Sorensen & Leonard, 2001].

### 5.3.7 Homo sapiens

One of the greatest evolutionary successes of Homo sapiens was the versatility and extent of their diet. Populations from late Pleistocene were hunter-gatherers who very well knew their surrounding and the natural cycle of plants and animals [Bae, 2013]. These proto-humans were aware that animals would move every season searching for new pastures. They knew the migration routes that animals used in each season, and they watched over them in order to attack the herds in unguarded and weak moments, planning their tactics in a sophisticated way to ensure hunting success [Bae, 2013].

The addition of new elements such as bones, antlers and ivory, along with the development of new technologies such as spears, arrows, bows, and traps, allowed Homo sapiens to expand their diet even more since they became able to hunt smaller animals, including marine animals. As their territory extended across the globe, they developed different food strategies according to the resources available in each region [Hancock *et al*, 2010].

Dissecting meat, dehydrating meat, freezing, smoking, preparing flesh and blood mixtures, fat mixtures, meat powder, fermenting products, and establishing "stores" on routes of annual or seasonal migration, might have been the best techniques to ensure survival. These practices allowed populations to permanently colonize areas where resources were scarce at some time of the year [Bae, 2013].

### 5.3.8 Food production in the Neolithic

In early of the Holocene* many landscapes changed. About 13 thousand years ago the last defrost began and the weather became more temperate and humid [Marcott *et al*, 2013]. The changing surrounding did not represent an abrupt change in the lifestyle. New human populations continued to live in the same territories and maintained the same type of diet to that of precedent communities [Smithsonian Institute].

The domestication of plants and animals represented a true revolution in human subsistence as it allowed the availability of a larger amount of food. New forms of agriculture and livestock farming consisted in the self-production of plant source and animal source foods, and occurred independently in several parts of the world [Weisdorf, 2005].

They began to gather grains in a selective manner to be able to plant and produce again. At the same time, they began to raise some animals inside the villages for their best use.

---

* The Holocene is a geological epoch which began at the end of the Pleistocene (at 11,700 calendar years BP) and continues to the present.

Germination and selection of grains and their subsequent cultivation, might have been discovered by observing the natural cycle of plants and intuitively reproducing it in order to get food [Weiss *et al*, 2006]. However, along with this new form of subsistence, wild animals hunting remained a complementary form of provisioning, as well as fishing and the gathering of fruit and uncropped vegetables [Biesalski *et al*, 2002]. Besides, thanks to domestication, new food products appeared, such as bread, wine, bear, and cheese. The discovery of how to produce them was probably accidental: by observing how accumulated surpluses of grains, fruits and milk spontaneously fermented [Berkowitz, 1996; Biesalski *et al*, 2002; Salque *et al*, 2012].

With the increase of food production, populations started to concentrate in certain places, and groups were created around certain resources. Sedentarization, therefore, started. Societies organized around villages and towns, which started to own certain resources and started to establish social relationships based on power and control over territories, either individual or familiar [Bocquet-Appel, 2008]. This brought along a demographic growth, confrontations over the control of food and differential access to it, as well as the emergence of some viral and deficiency diseases (such as vitamin deficiency, scurvy, beriberi, and pellagra) and hunger in periods of scarcity [Armelagos *et al*, 1991; Furuse *et al*, 2010].

### 5.3.9 An increasingly varied diet

In the course of human evolution, diet has been

increasingly diverse thanks to the addition of new nutrients to the basic plant component and to increasingly complex technical systems.

About 12 thousand years ago the first great technological revolution related to food occurred and allowed men to control the production of their food. Currently, we are living a new technological revolution in the field of biotechnology. Progress that has been done on new techniques applied to food allow us to alter their composition in order to improve their nutritional qualities (adding omega-3 fatty acids, increasing calcium content, reducing cholesterol content, etcetera) or to simply make them more appetizing by endowing them with attractive colors or enhancing their flavor.

With the above-mentioned, I wanted to expose the mistake that is made when referring to a vegetarian diet as something natural for human beings, and therefore as something good that must be done. Humans are neither carnivorous nor vegetarian nor fruitarian by nature, our physiology and our anatomy indicate that we are in the middle: we are omnivores.

However, the statement "we are omnivores" has some implications. Some take it as a synonym of that we need and/or must consume animal source foods because that is what our nature dictates. This assumption is as erroneous as the other, because our omnivorous nature indicates that we have the capacity of eating everything, not that we must do so. It is up to us whether to do it or not, and as we saw in previous chapters, a vegetarian diet meets the nutritional requirements of all age groups.

Besides, not few fall into to the Fallacy of Tradition (argumentum ad antiquitatem) by saying that we must consume meat because we have always done so. If anything characterizes human beings that is their capacity to adapt and their ingenuity to develop technologies that will allow them to fulfill their needs. As mentioned by the anthropologist PhD. William Leonard in an article from 2002: *"We now know that humans have evolved not to subsist on a single paleolithic diet but to be flexible eaters, an insight that has important implications for the current debate over what people today should eat in order to be healthy."* [Leonard, 2002]. Thereby, deterministic arguments regarding the nature of human diet are fallacious.

### 5.4 It is not natural to consume milk

Many vegetarians, with the intention of inducing a decrease of milk consumption in the population, tend to fall into the error of stating that "human beings are the only animals that continue to consume milk after weaning, therefore, we should not do it because it is not natural".

Although the data is correct (we are the only animals that continue to consume milk after weaning), once again we incur in the naturalistic fallacy of this not being natural to happen, and therefore being wrong. Besides, there are some reasons to consider that it is natural for human beings to continue their milk consumption (in any of its forms) after weaning.

Lactase is an enzyme that is synthesized in the cells lining the wall of the small intestine. It has fundamental function in the digestion of milk sugar (lactose). Normally, this enzyme is synthesized by human beings during the breastfeeding stage.

In some cases, the synthesis of this enzyme in the intestinal wall stops when lactation is over, generally causing a condition known as lactose intolerance, very common in populations of African, Asian and Native American ethnic origin [NIH, 2012]. But some groups can continue to consume lactose-containing products without any problems, because the enzyme continues to be synthesized. This is a condition known as lactase persistence, which is a persistent production of the lactase enzyme during adulthood. Research suggests that this is a result of a mutation that happened more than 75 hundred years ago somewhere in Europe, a mutation of the allele, where the gene in charge of synthetizing the lactase enzyme is found [Itan et al, 2009; Leonardia et al, 2012].

Some authors have proposed that this mutation was beneficial for populations that lived in the Northern Europe region where sunlight exposure is scarce, because milk is a product with good concentrations of calcium and vitamin D, both fundamental compounds for the healthy development of bones [Flatz & Rotthauwe, 1973].

With the pressure of natural selection, those with the mutation were favored. For that reason, it seems like people with European ancestors maintain the mutation and the condition of lactase persistence, which allows them to consume dairy products without suffering the gastrointestinal problems that derive from the absence of this enzyme.

The increase in the consumption of dairy that occurred about 75 hundred years ago was due to this fact, and happened in the same evolutionary frame than the development of the opposable thumb or the increase in the size of the brain, for instance. Natural selection and evolution have endowed certain populations with the capacity of consuming milk-derived products after weaning. From this we can infer that consuming milk during adulthood is something natural, but that does not mean that we should do so (naturalistic fallacy).

## 5.5 The paleodiet or paleolithic diet

Even though this subject has nothing to do with vegetarianism, I will take advantage of what has been stated above regarding the evolution of the human diet, to demystify a dietary regime that is making a lot of noise in the media and in the general population.

In September of 2013, an article published in the newspaper Infobae commented on this diet, its history, the opening of a restaurant in Recoleta* and, obviously, famous people that followed it [Blanco, 2013]. Basically, the paleolithic diet, caveman diet or Stone Age diet, is a nutritional regime based on foods that were supposedly consumed by humans during the Paleolithic period. The diet focuses on the consumption of foods that were apparently available at the time. It consists mainly of meat, fish, fruits, vegetables, dry fruits, and roots; and it excludes grains, legumes, dairy, salt, refined sugar, and processed oils. It rejects all derivatives of the agricultural and industrial revolution.

---

*   Recoleta is a downtown residential neighborhood in the Autonomous City of Buenos Aires, Argentina. It is one of the most affluent neighborhoods and it is one of the priciest real estate in the city.

It argues that the anatomy, physiology and genetics of modern humans practically have not changed since the Paleolithic period, thus there is a conflict between our body and our current diet, which causes obesity, myocardial infarction, diabetes, cancer and other "modern" diseases. So says PhD. Loren Coridain, specialist in exercise physiology and founder of the paleo movement, in his articles "Biological and clinical potential of a paleolithic diet" [Lindeberg *et al*, 2003] and "Origins and evolution of the Western diet: health implications for the 21st century" [Cordain *et al*, 2005].

It seems like this diet attempts to have a scientific basis, but its underlying logic fails on several points: it divinizes one period of our evolutionary history, it insists on us being biologically the same to humans from more than 10 thousand years ago, it denies the benefits of some modern feeding methods, and it incurs into the naturalistic fallacy of "going back to basics". Based on that, I dare to say that it is just another trendy diet and that we could include it on the list of pseudosciences.

### 5.5.1 Paleodiet does not exist

As I described in the section on the evolution of the human diet, it is clear that the diet that Homo sapiens had before the agricultural revolution depended exclusively on the available food and on the ingenuity of proto-humans to take advantage of it. So, the diet of populations from Europe was different from those of America, Asia or the Pacific Islands.

It is also hard to establish what we mean by "Paleolithic",

because this term is no longer used within the sciences that study men, and only its vestiges remain in the popular knowledge. Anthropology and archeology refer to the lifestyles of societies independently from place and time, which is the reason why nowadays there are societies have a Paleolithic lifestyle (gatherers and hunters).

## 5.5.2 We are no our ancestors

The idea of that we have not changed genetically does not take into account the latest research on evolution nor the new studies on genetics. There are several examples of recent human evolutionary changes that happened relatively fast. One example of this is the above-mentioned lactase persistence. Another example of this is the mutation of the gene for blue eyes, which could have happened between 6 and 10 thousand years ago [Eiberg *et al*, 2008]. Also, it has been found that the immune system and the red blood cells from people that live in areas of endemic malaria have been modified in a way that helps the body fight the disease, which is transmitted by mosquitoes. Some of these mutations were originated 5 or 10 thousand years ago [Kwiatkowski, 2005].

Even microorganisms we share our bodies with have evolved faster, especially bacteria that live in our intestines and help us digest food, which makes every microbiome different. Although we do not have direct evidence of the bacterial species that lived in our intestines during the Paleolithic, we can be fairly certain that they were different from the current ones [Dethlefsen *et al*, 2005; Ley *et al*, 2008].

### 5.5.3 Food has also changed

Plants and animals we feed ourselves with have also evolved. Food sources that existed more than 10 thousand years ago were very different from the current ones. Most of them have been modified by artificial selection: corn was a grass called teosinte, tomatoes evolved from simple berries, cows were domesticated and modified from wild aurochs 9 thousand years ago, and cabbage, broccoli, cauliflower, brussels sprouts, and kale are all different varieties from the same species (*Brassica oleracea*).

It is needless to say that some of the animals that were consumed then do not exist today, like the mammoth.

### 5.5.4 Our ancestors were not healthier

Those who defend the paleodiet not only do not understand our own species, (microorganisms that inhabit us and food sources have evolved in the last 10 thousand years), but they also ignore the evidence on the health of our ancestors during their brief lives [Caspari & Lee, 2004]. Those who follow a paleodiet assume that atherosclerosis is a disease linked to a modern lifestyle, and that if human beings emulated a preindustrial lifestyle or even a pre-agricultural lifestyle, atherosclerosis or at least its clinical manifestations would be avoided [Cordain *et al*, 2005]. However, Thomson and colleagues recently searched for signs of atherosclerosis and artery blockage by cholesterol and fat, in more than a thousand mummies from ancient agricultural societies, gatherers and hunter-gatherers worldwide (Egypt, Peru, Southwestern United States and Aleutian Islands). They found proof of the presence of atherosclerosis in 47 out of 137 mummies of each of the different geographical regions [Thompson *et al*, 2013].

A clear example of why hunter-gatherer societies were not healthier than our society is, is provided in a study published by Hill and colleagues, which analyzed the high mortality of the Hiwi tribe and its implications in the understanding of human evolution. This work questioned what was known about the mortality of ancient hunter-gatherer societies [Hill *et al*, 2006]. The Hiwi society lives in the Neotropical Savanna around the Orinoco River (Venezuela), and subsists by gathering and hunting a diverse group of plants and animals that the jungle, the pentane and the rivers provide (similar to the Paleolithic culture). Their main sources of meat were capybaras, collared peccaries, deers, anteaters, armadillos, numerous species of fish, and at least some species of turtle. They consumed roots (bitter and sweet), palm nuts and palm hearts, various types of fruit, a wild legume called *Campsiandra comosa*, and honey produced by several species of bee. The authors found that Hiwis were not particularly healthy: only 51% of children older than 10 years could reach an age of 40 years, and the majority of people were infected with parasites.

*5.5.5 Unsubstantiated statements*

Some of the most interesting things about the paleodiet, which label it as a pseudoscience, are its statements regarding the functioning of the body, found on the official website of the paleo movement [The Paleo Diet].

The sixth item from the tab "Premise" on its website,

exposes the pseudoscientific nature of the paleodiet. It reads "Net dietary alkaline load that balances dietary acid". They assume that certain types of food acidify the body, and that food they recommend alkalize the body, making it healthier. Besides, body acidification leads to calcium loss through urine and predisposes to kidney stones. Both statements are entirely false and both topics we have discussed a few pages back.

What is being criticized is not the diet itself, because there is a lack of studies to draw conclusions on its effects, but the theoretical frame on which it is sustained, which is absurd and has no scientific evidence backing it up, apart from its pseudoscientific nature.

Some may say that it works and that they do well on this diet, but that would be another analysis, because that result can be explained by many other factors that are proven to have an impact on health, such as eliminating the consumption of processed and refined food or increasing the consumption of fruits and vegetables [CDC, 2013].

In summary, we can say that all of the foundations of the paleolithic diet are false. We are not like our ancestors nor were they healthier. There was not a single paleolithic diet, but Homo sapiens were characterized by their eating flexibility. And even if it existed we would not be able to emulate it, because plants and animals that lived in the Planet more that 10 million years ago have completely changed.

# Conclusions

*Translation: Federico Palacín*

We are facing an uncertain future: The natural resources and the ecosystems that support us are collapsing at an unsettling rate, and we are doing nothing to prevent this trend from actually happening. We are driving towards a "suicide on a grand scale" (as Prince Charles mentioned) [Brown, 2012], or as (UK Chief Scientific Advisor) Prof. John Beddington, PhD, calls it, the "perfect storm" of environmental issues [Sample, 2009].

In 1972, Meadows and colleagues published the book "The Limits to Growth", which describes through computing modeling analysis, the exponential behavior of the economic and the global population growth in an environment with limited supply of resources (trend observed for decades) [Meadows *et al*, 1972]. While this book did not intend to make predictions, their results showed conclusively; that if we continue with these current trends of resource-use, we will suffer an imminent collapse with a subsequent reduction of the population by famine.

The book was criticized by their peers, arguing that it was based "only" on computing modeling. A research comparing the data provided by "The Limits of Growth" with data from the last 30 years, was published in 2008, and concluded that the exhibited trends are following the course predicted by the authors. This certainly, reinforces the idea of a possible economic collapse at mid-century, by different causes [Turner, 2008].

Around March of 2014, a study called "Human and Nature Dynamics" (HANDY) was published by the National Socio-Environmental Synthesis Center from USA (SESYNC), and was sponsored by NASA [Motesharrei et al, 2014]. The research led by Safa Motesharre, PhD, in collaboration with specialists in atmospheric and political sciences, analyses the collapse of ancient civilizations and raises questions about the sustainability of modern civilization. Montesharrei built a mathematical model to explore the interaction between population and natural resources dynamics. He attempted to develop a simulated scenario in which social collapse can be avoided by taking into account the carrying capacity of the earth. He mentioned "population can reach a steady state at maximum carrying capacity if the rate of depletion of nature is reduced to a sustainable level and if resources are distributed equitably". The study concludes that an urgent general approach is necessary because the current situation of our civilization (over-exploitation of natural resources and strong social-economic stratification) can independently produce the suitable setting for a complete collapse.

Climate change could be in fact, one of the most serious issues we are facing. However other factors could also contribute to the collapse, such as: an accelerated extinction of animal and vegetal species that could lead to a loss of essential services for the survival of human ecosystems, land overuse and degradation, acidification and eutrophication of oceans (dead zones); increasing depletion of scarce resources, including (mainly) underground water, which are being polluted and over-exploited in many key agricultural areas; and armed conflicts [Ehrlich & Ehrlich, 2013].

These should not be approached as separate issues, because they belong to larger and more complex interacting systems, like the biosphere and human socio-economic systems. The future of livestock and environment will be determined by the way in which the balance between these two competing demands is being settled: On one hand, the demand for food of animal origin; and on the other hand, the demand for environmental services. Both are driven by population growth and increased consumption, as key factors.

Summarizing key points:

1.  Growth for animal source foods demand in the coming decades will be remarkable. Even though the annual growth rate will be relatively lower than in past decades, growth in absolute volume will be larger. The estimated per capita meat consumption in 2050 will be

about 49,4 kg/person/year, if the population growth continues up to the estimated amount (9 billion people by 2050), the meat production should increase to 455 million tones, almost twice the current production [Alexandratos & Bruinsma, 2012].

2. Hunger strikes 868 million people, and constitutes a major health problem, even greater than HIV, malaria and tuberculosis combined [WFP, 2013].

3. Food production increased between 70% and 280% since 1960 [Rudela *et al*, 2009; Royal Society, 2009]

4. We are producing, at present, enough food to offer at least 2720 Kcal/person/day, to the entire world population [FAO, 2002].

5. 35% of the global grain production in 2013 was used to feed cattle; including 19% of wheat and 57% of coarse grains (sorghum, millet, oats, rye and barley) [FAO, 2014]. While, the 97% of the soybean meal world production it is generally assigned to feed production for monogastric species, especially poultry and pigs, to a lesser extent [Steinfeld *et al*, 2006].

6. In 2013, the use of feed grains was 858.2 million tons and projections for 2050 estimate approximately 1.113 billion tons [FAO, 2014; Alexandratos & Bruinsma, 2012].

7. It takes 7 to 32,8 kg of grain to produce 1 kg of meat, depending on the type of meat (beef, swine, sheep and sausages) [Friedl *et al*, 2007; UNCCD, 2009].

8. Between 26% and 45% of the world's surface is occupied by livestock systems, while 33% of the world's arable land is used to produce livestock feed [Steinfeld *et al*, 2006; Thornton *et al*, 2011].

9. At present, 31% of the land surface is covered by forests, approximately 9 billion hectares [FAO, 2010].

10. Between 65-80% of Amazon deforestation is destined to produce croplands for cattle feed [Wassenaar *et al*, 2007; Nepstad *et al*, 2008; May *et al*; 2010].

11. If current trends in agricultural exploitation continue in Brazil, approximately 40% of the Amazon forest watershed will be deforested by 2050 [Soares-Filh *et al*, 2006].

12. In Argentina, only 30% of the native forest that existed 100 years ago remain [UMSEF, 2007].

13. The main cause of deforestation in Argentina is the advance of the agricultural frontier and mostly soybean cultivation in the recent years [UMSEF, 2012].

14. In Cordoba Province, less than 10% of its native forests are left. Agriculture and livestock have been the main responsible for this deforestation [Cabido & Zak, 2010].

15. The Government has launched the Agro-Food and Agro-Industrial Strategic Plan (ASP), whose goal is to increase meat and grain production. A requirement of 9 to 20 million hectares is estimated, almost between 50% and 100% of the native forests current remaining area [Merenson, 2011; PEA, 2013].

16. In 2004, the GEO report mentioned: *"It must be considered that if the country wants to reach 100 million tons in grain, the agricultural frontier would have to be extended to almost 12 to 15 million ha, inferring that the maintenance of the current extension of native forests, would be in danger"* [GEO, 2004, p92].

17. At present time, agriculture is using 70% of the blue water (rivers and aquifers) [FAO, 2011].

18. The water demand needed to produce 1kg of animal product is 15410 liters/kg, mutton 10410 liters/kg, pork 5980 liters/kg, goat meat 5500 liters/kg and chicken 4320 liters/kg [Mekonnen & Hoekstra, 2012].

19. There will not be enough water available for productive cropland to produce food for the expected population by 2050 if we continue with current trends towards diets

based on animal origin food (3000 kcal/day, of which 20-30% is animal protein). However, there will be enough water if the proportion of animal source food is limited to 5% of total calories [SIWI, 2012].

20. The amount of manure produced by livestock is a major cause of water dead zones and eutrophication [NRDC, 2013a].

21. Livestock produce biological water pollution and is responsible for the high antibiotic resistance of most bacteria [Hudson, 2008; Marshall & Levy, 2011, CDC, 2013].

22. Cattle grazing degrades the soil through the mechanical action of hooves, subsequently causing disturbances in watersheds [USFWS, 2009].

23. In several areas of Argentina, the livestock industry has had a negative impact on watershed due to the unlimited land-use for grazing [Facelli *et al*, 1988; Palacio *et al*, 2014].

24. 83% of the land in Sierras Grandes of Córdoba is assigned to traditional continuous high load livestock husbandry, thereby exhibiting high levels of soil erosion and degradation [Cingolani *et al*, 2003].

25. abaquillo trees are essential to ensure adequately the

function of watersheds in Sierras Grandes of Córdoba. However, intensive regrowth grazing prevents their normal growth, keeping them always small, thereby reducing the recovering possibility of Tabaquillo forests [Giorgis *et al*, 2010; Marcora *et al*, 2013].

26. Global warming is an undeniable fact. Its existence is recognized by 97% of the climate scientists and leading scientific institutions in the world [JSAS, 2010; Cook *et al*, 2013; IPCC, 2013].

27. The livestock sector, mainly meat and milk industry, is responsible for 14,5% of the greenhouse gases emission from anthropogenic origin [Gerber *et al*, 2013].

28. Almost 1.4 billion people worldwide are overweight or obese. This disease is becoming a pandemic and constitutes a serious public health issue. It is related to many chronic diseases, and also represents the largest risk factor for cancer [Wyatt *et al*, 2006; WHO, 2013; De Pergola & Silvestris, 2013].

29. Numerous studies have linked meat consumption with obesity or overweight due to (probably) a higher intake of total fat, saturated fat, total calories and a reduction in the consumption of vegetables [Vang *et al*, 2008; Wang & Beydoun, 2009].

30. The most important nutritional institutions worldwide

agree that vegetarian diets, even the more strict ones, are nutritionally adequate for all stages of life, and even suitable for athletes [Craig & Mangels, 2009; AEDN, 2009; ACS, 2010; Amit, 2010; Garton, 2011; Dietitians of Canada, 2013; AAP, 2013].

31. Vegetarians have lower rates of obesity, overweight, type 2 diabetes, cardiovascular disease, hypertension, and colon cancer. In addition, a vegetarian diet can help in other digestive disorders such as constipation and diverticulosis/diverticulitis [Craig & Mangels, 2009].

The arguments and figures provided by previous researches showed clearly that a meat-based diet is inefficient from a resource-use point of view; and that is something we should not ignore. Although this production system is inherently inefficient, these conclusive data bring us to the idea that, perhaps, these problems could not be solved by simply improving the production chain.

If these current trends continue, it would cause a collapse, and they must be reversed towards a more positive direction. The economic and population growth combined with the increasing scarcity of natural resources, together with the worsening environmental problems; are producing an increased demand for environmental services. This demand will be expanded over and over again: from the immediate factors of concern, such as the inconvenience caused by odors; through intermediate demands for water and clean air; to wider and longer-term environmental concerns, such as climate change or irreversible loss of biodiversity, among others.

If a radical remedial action is absent, the environmental impact of livestock production will worsen dramatically. Stated simply, if production is doubled without the subsequent reduction of environmental impacts per unit of production, environmental damage will double.

Therefore I will state my position clearly: I do not consider adopting a vegetarian diet will save us from environmental collapse. There are many factors at play. The economic system is the most important and should be modified if we aspire to long-term benefits. But there is no doubt in the fact that the widespread adoption of a vegetarian diet (in all its variants) or, even, a significant decrease in the consumption of meat and animal products per person per year, would mean a great help when facing the problems mentioned throughout this book.

Below, I will discuss the same questions that were exposed on chapter "Economy and Food Security":

- Are there suitable amounts of water and land enough to enlarge the farming and grazing surfaces? Or are these vital resources in short supply?
- Is there a margin to obtain higher agricultural performance? Or are we reaching the maximum soil exploitation?

- Can biotechnology provide a new crop generation suitable for the environment and greater performance?
- And lastly, are there any plans for agriculture to be able to increase production while improving ecosystems conservation?

If we continue with the current consumption trends and fulfill the predictions of increased consumption of animal source foods by 2050, the first question results negative. We must remember that we live on this planet and we do not have yet, the ability to use resources that do not exist here. Water should be a priority, as agriculture is the sector with the highest water consumption, adjustments and improvements should be made in the production chain; and blaming people for water use at homes should be avoided.

There are lands to continue the production growth, but these lands are now forests, jungles, grasslands and other intact ecosystems. The advance of the agricultural frontier threatens the ecosystem services provided by these areas on which we depend so much.

The second and third questions are a possibility. Probably, biotechnology is one of the tools that we can count on to save us from the environmental collapse that we are causing. Climate change will have serious consequences for agriculture, and the development of seeds adapted to new climatic requirements will be essential to maintain the security of food supply. However, a recent article by Grassini and colleagues published in the journal Nature, warns that industrial agriculture may have reached its limits in the production of staple crops for mankind, and is not able to feed the growing world population [Grassini *et al*, 2013]. They also exposed the current lack of production growth of major crops, contradicting the optimistic speech of the rising productivity expressed by the grain companies.

I fully understand that meat consumption is related to deeply rooted cultural values in some societies, but we are talking about our survival as a species. Science, once again, has given us evidence for this situation in which we find ourselves, and although these data will probably be amended over time, the trend seems evident.

We need to rethink the way in which we relate to nature, and which are the most feasible solutions to address these problems; which we will meet soon. We are not talking about trivial problems, but problems that can actually endanger the world's population, especially the poorest and most vulnerable.

Again, I do not think vegetarianism is the divine salvation, but I do consider it can help us a lot to establish new policies for food production that will bring us benefits in the way we use the finite natural resources. I would like to emphasize that I am not asking to go back to the 15th century or start producing our food. If we deny the scientific and technological advances we will be choosing the wrong path. Technology is a tool and like any tool, it has no morals, the results of its application depend entirely on the way in which we use it. Therefore, we should rethink the way in which we will use science and technology, and it should be for achieving benefits on our long-term survival, not to benefit our pockets.

We should begin to consider the idea of reducing our meat and animal source foods consumption because we simply do not have many more options. Although new technologies in the food industry are aiming to develop in vitro meat (lab-grown meat) [Jha, 2013]; it seems quite unlikely that these techniques could be capable of producing over 300 million tonnes of meat per year, but maybe I am wrong.

Governments should promote policies to encourage dietary change, develop guidelines with dietary recommendations, subsidizing the production of fruits and vegetables, and reducing or eliminating subsidies to the livestock sector. They should also promote education campaigns aiming at agricultural producers to understand the implications of their activities on the environment at the same time they should develop plans of action to improve irrigation technologies to improve efficiency in the use of water. I also understand that to reduce/eliminate subsidies to the livestock sector in countries that have an export model such as Argentina, Brazil and Uruguay, seem a utopia; a significant percentage of the gross domestic product of these countries comes from agricultural production.

Another interesting idea would be to tax on meat production so that the money collected could be redistributed to other sectors such as Education, Health or Science. Meat should be considered as a luxury product and it should be pricey (more than now), since its production is costly in environmental terms. The thought *"Those who want meat, should pay it dearly"* sounds reasonable, then we could achieve a reduction in meat consumption and redistribute the surplus to benefit priority sectors and activities. It should be emphasized that honest and transparent rulers would be necessary; unfortunately they are considered endangered specimens.

I am beating around the bush, I am certainly not qualified to address this issue. The development of political strategies is a very complex topic and requires an interdisciplinary professional interaction from different areas; such sociologist, biologist, agronomists, physicians and politics scientists.

If we contemplate for a moment the consequences of the decrease in animal source foods consumption, we would conclude that it could bring us enormous benefits in terms of health and environmental perspective. As discussed in Chapter 4, vegetarian diets could be a powerful weapon in the prevention of common chronic diseases such as obesity, metabolic syndrome, type 2 diabetes and cardiovascular disease, thus, constituting a major weapon for public health.

According to the perspective of this book, the environmental benefit should be the most interesting issue to be addressed. By these lines I guess the reader should agree that the livestock sector needs many resources, including land. Reducing the consumption of animal source foods, made by this sector, will inevitably lead to a decline in the use of soil for grazing and grain cultivation. Stehfest and colleagues estimated that the widespread adoption of a vegetarian diet would result in the abandonment of over 2.7 billion hectares of pasture and 100 million hectares of farmland [Stehfest *et al*, 2009]. Such space could be used for ecosystem restoration projects.

Ecosystem restoration (or ecological restoration) is defined as "*the process of assisting the recovery of an ecosystem that has been degraded, damaged or destroyed*" [IUCN, 2012]. There are many cases of environmental degradation, some have been revised throughout this book, the most common caused by logging, overgrazing, damming rivers, hurricanes, floods and fires [Vaughn *et al*, 2010]; therefore, it is interesting to imagine the possible application of this (relatively new) science in regions where livestock and agriculture have caused damage, and without human intervention, they would be destined to a complete collapse.

I will quote a local example of ecological restoration, which deserves recognition. Is the one that Daniel Renison, PhD, has being carrying out by for over 16 years in Macizo Los Gigantes of Sierras Grandes from Córdoba (Argentina). Renison, together with colleagues, evaluated the effects of livestock exclusion (by wire) and reforestation with native trees (Polylepis australis) in degraded areas. For this he used 2 sites of about 20 hectares each presenting the same bioclimatic conditions. He excluded livestock in one area and carried out reforestation, and in the other area, he did not. The results suggest that the intervention improved water recharge in the area with livestock exclusion [Renison *et al*, 2005; Landi & Renison, 2010; Lazzarini, 2013].

We will be highly benefitted from the climatic point of view as well. As it was previously mentioned, most scientists have agreed for years, that climate change is the main environmental problem we are facing and that we must address it immediately [Thomas *et al*, 2003; Lobell *et al*, 2008; Smitha *et al*, 2009; Ehrlich & Ehrlich, 2013]. In this context many authors suggest that a modification in food patterns could be remarkably helpful in the control of climate change. Unfortunately this is a very poorly explored field in climate policies. Carlsson-Kanyama and Gonzalez confirmed greenhouse gas emission coming from plant-based foods is much smaller compared with the emission from animal-based foods production; being 0,42-2,3 kg $CO_2$ equivalent/kg for the first group and 2,5-3 for the latter (greenhouse gasses are measured in carbon dioxide equivalences according to their capacity to retain heat) [Carlsson-Kanyama & González, 2009]. Stehfest and colleagues estimated that the massive adoption of an lacto-ovo vegetarian diet would significantly reduce the greenhouse gases emission from agricultural industry by the year 2050: carbon dioxide by 17%, methane by 24% and nitrous oxide by 21%, stabilizing at 450ppm of CO2 equivalent for that year [Stehfest *et al*, 2009]. Thus, in agreement with other authors, Popp and colleagues consider that the change in dietary patterns are more important than technology implementations to mitigate climate change [McMichael *et al*, 2007; Friel *et al*, 2009; Garnett, 2009; Popp *et al*, 2010]. The impact would be so dramatic that Hedenus and colleagues considered recently that a shift to diets with less meat and dairy is essential to achieve with a high probability of success, the objective of 2° C proposed by the United Nations Environment Programme (UNEP) [Hedenus *et al*, 2014].

We must not forget the contribution that vegetarian diets can make to food security, related to food availability and environmental improvement, as mentioned above. The decrease in meat consumption would cause a reduction in the amount of feed grain and food could be produced for those people who really need them; and release lands to cultivate foods for direct human consumption [Stokstad, 2010; ICD, 2013]. Cassidy and colleagues recently demonstrated that adopting a vegetarian diet would increase the grain conversion efficiency up to 35% and thus increase the food availability to 815 million more people [Cassidy *et al*, 2013]. While Foley and colleagues estimated that if the 16 most cultivated grains redirected entirely to human food, supply would increase by more than a billion tonnes and calories by 49% [Foley *et al*, 2011].

If this is not enough, a recently published study conducted by Eshela and colleagues, attempted to quantify the resources needed per unit of nutrient (megacalorie) for the five most consumed animal source foods in the United States: milk, meat, poultry, pork, and eggs [Eshela *et al*, 2014]. The results were:

- 0.6 million $km^2$ of land are used for forage, which represents 40% of the arable land in the United States ($2000 \ m^2$ per person).
- If we add to that number the area occupied by

grasslands, it hikes up to 3.7 million km$^2$, which represents 40% of the entire area of the United States.

- It takes 45 billion m$^3$ of water to irrigate fodder crops, accounting for 27% of the total water used for irrigation.
- 6 million metric tons of nitrogen fertilizer are used for crops, and that alone accounts for 5% of the entire greenhouse gases emissions in the country.

The authors acknowledge that despite many investigations have been conducted, few changes have occurred in the political and individual consumption habits.

Although individual dietary changes are the beginning, it is certainly not enough if the aim is to produce a significant and organized change, which could endure over time. I insist that population in general, in addition to diet changing, should pressure governments to make them listen to adopt these measures. To expect problems to be solved by magic is no longer an option. We know the causes of these problems and we have the possible answers and approaches on how to address them.

As discussed throughout this book, we know the causes of problems and approaches on how we address them.

The scientific knowledge provided in the last 200 years of our history in this universe is gorgeous. Actually we are very lucky to be here. There have been unlikely circumstances for billions of years to reach this eminent and distinguished position in nature. We do not really know how we got to this point because we do not know very well when we started doing the things that characterize us.

But what we really know, is that our survival on this planet is in our hands, and it no longer depends on just lucky breaks as when an asteroid collided with the Earth 4.5 billion years ago, which determined the origin of the moon and stabilized the Earth's axis; or the extinction of the dinosaurs 65 million years ago, allowing mammals to be the dominant species of the world. Although this survival era we are facing, goes far beyond from what we eat or do not eat. Diet change, putting pressure on governments and informing the rest of society about a reality that concerns all of us, is actually a great kickoff.

It is not the intention of this book, to give answers to all the questions that may have arisen. Nor do I consider that my opinions are valid; because, as I mentioned earlier, I am not qualified in political, economic, ecological, agronomical, and nutritional fields. I have researched rigorously and have encouraged myself to share what I consider personally, is a socially relevant issue. With the intention of introducing vegetarianism within the political debate; I actually think that through vegetarianism, interesting contributions can be made, and urgent problems can be solved.

If there is anything that characterizes us as human beings is our ability to adapt to the new challenges posed by the environment and the inventiveness when solving problems. Another kind of diet can be adopted; one that could supply our nutritional requirements perfectly, while we can help to eliminate, at the same time, the cause of some state of affairs that are threatening our survival on Earth.

I am still optimistic and I really hope you are too.

 *Appendix*

**Figure 1:** "The Great Chaco" (El Gran Chaco)

*Gran Chaco. The World Factbook de la CIA.*

Very approximate location of the Gran Chaco (underlying map taken from the CIA World Factbook).

**Image extracted from:**
http://es.wikipedia.org/wiki/Gran_Chaco#mediaviewer/File:GranChacoApproximate.jpg

**Figure 2:** Political map of Argentine Republic

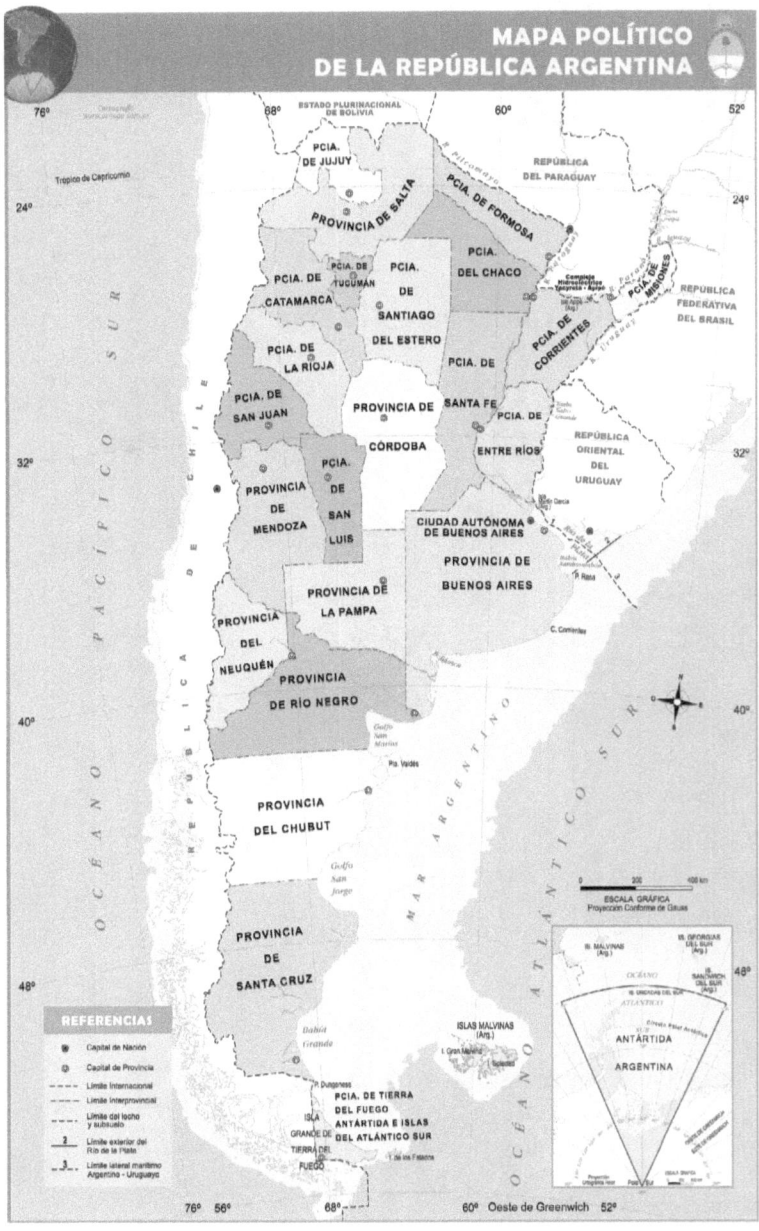

**Image extracted from:**
- Mapa poítico de la República Argentina. Mapoteca,
Programa Educar, Ministerio de Educación, Gobierno de
la República Argentina.
Available online at:
http://mapoteca.educ.ar/mapa/republica-argentina/

**Figure 3:** Map of eco-regions of the Argentina Republic

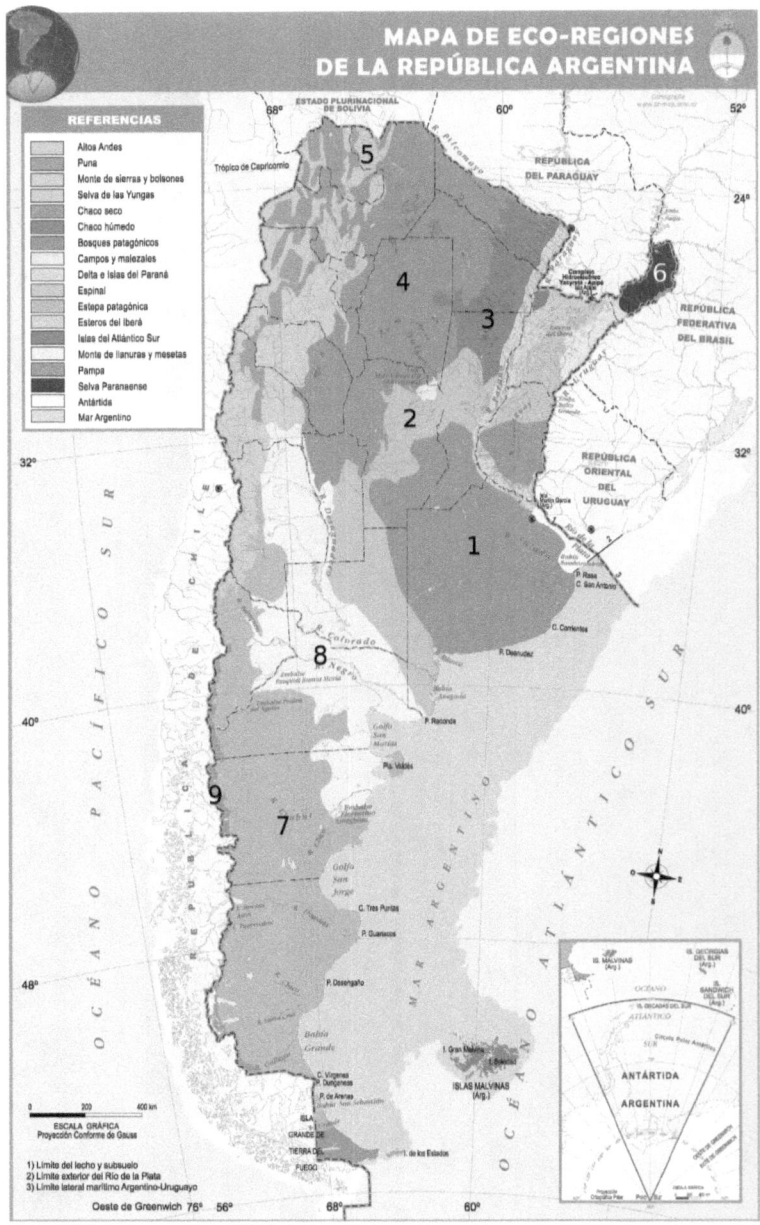

**References:**
1) Humid Pampa (Pampa Húmeda)
2) (Espinal)
3) Chaco Húmedo
4) Chaco Seco
5) Selva de los Yungas
6) Selva Paranaense
7) Estepa patagónica
8) Montes de llanuras y mesetas
9) Bosques patagónicos

**Image extracted from:**
- Eco-regiones de la República Argentina. Mapoteca, Programa Educar, Ministerio de Educación, Gobierno de la República Argentina.
Available online at:
http://mapoteca.educ.ar/mapa/republica-argentina/

**Figure 4:** Physical map of the province of Cordoba

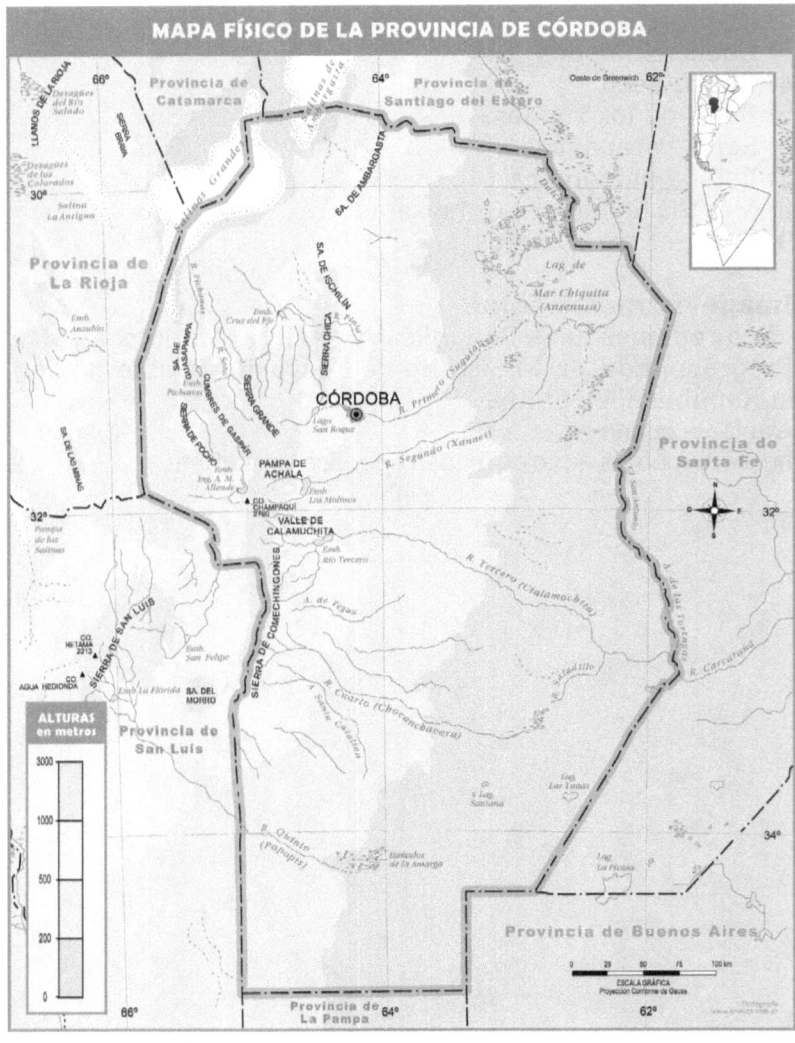

**Image extracted from:**
- Mapa físico de la Provincia de Córdoba (Argentina).
Mapoteca, Programa Educar, Ministerio de Educación,
Gobierno de la República Argentina.
Available online at: http://mapoteca.educ.ar/mapa/cordoba/

# B    *Bibliography*

## Chapter 1: "Introduction"

FAO & Biodiversity International, (2012). Sustainable Diets and Biodiversity: Directions and solutions for policy, research and action. Food and Agriculture Organization of the United Nations (FAO). Rome, Italy.

FAO, (2010). Final Report. Scientific Symposium "Biodiversity and Sustainable Diets". Food and Agriculture Organization of the United Nations. Rome, Italy.

Magee L, Scerri A, James P, Thom JA, Padgham L, Hickmott S, Deng H, Cahill F, (2013). Reframing social sustainability reporting: towards an engaged approach. Environ Dev Sustain 15: 225-243.

NIH, (2014). Vegetarian diet. U. S. National Library of Medicine [in line]. May 2014. [Accessed Jylu 25, 2014]. Available online at: http://www.nlm.nih.gov/medlineplus/vegetariandiet.html

Steinfeld H, Gerber P, Wassenaar T, Castel V, Rosales M, de Haan C, (2006). Livestock's Long

Shadow: Environmental issues and options. FAO/LEAD, Rome, Italy.

UNEP, (2012). Avoiding Future Famines: Strengthening the Ecological Foundation of Food Security through Sustainable Food Systems. United Nations Environment Programme (UNEP), Nairobi, Kenya.

Vegan Society, (2013). Memoradum of Association of The Vegan Society [in line]. November 1979. [Accessed December 22, 2013]. Available online at:

http://www.vegansociety.com/pdf/ArticlesofAssociation.pdf

Vegetarian Society, (2013). FAQ's about vegetarianism [in line]. [Accessed December 22, 2013]. Available online at:
 https://www.vegsoc.org/FAQs#.Urdbp46zDgU

**Chapter 2: "Economy and Food Security"**

Abel-Smith B, Leiserson A, (1978). Pobreza, desarrollo y políticas de salud. Organización Mundial de la Salud. Ginebra, Suiza.

Ag-Info Center, (2014). How Much Feed Will My Cow Eat - Frequently Asked Questions. Alberta Ag-Info Center, Alberta Agriculture and Rural Development [in line]. November 2013. [Accessed December 26, 2013]. Available online at:
http://www1.agric.gov.ab.ca/
$department/deptdocs.nsf/all/faq7811?opendocument

Alexandratos N, Bruinsma J, (2012). World agriculture towards 2030/2050: the 2012 revision. ESA Working paper No. 12-03. Rome, Italy.

APAARI, (2012). Regional Consultation on Improving Wheat Productivity in Asia. Asia Pacific Association of Agricultural Research Institutions [in line]. Abril 2012. [Accessed December 24, 2013]. Available online at: http://www.apaari.org/events/wheatcon12.html

Asner GP, Elmore AJ, Olander LP, Martin RE, Harris AT, (2004). Grazyng systems, ecosystem responses and global change. Annu Rev Environ Resour 29: 261-299.

Bryce J, Coitinho D, Darnton-Hill I, Pelletier D, Pinstrup-Andersen P, (2008). Maternal and child undernutrition: effective action at national level. The Lancet; 371(9611): 510-526.

Cicchino M, Otondo J, Melani E, Bailleres MA, (2012). SORGO: Ensayo comparativo de rendimiento para silaje planta entera - Campaña 2012/2013 . Instituto Nacional de Tecnología Agropecuaria (INTA) y Ministerio de Asuntos Agrarios de la Provincia de Buenos Aires (MAA). Buenos Aires, Argentina.

CreditLoan, (2011). Food Consumption in America [in line]. December 2011. [Accessed December 28, 2013]. Available online at:

http://www.creditloan.com/blog/food-consumption-in-america/

Cromwell GL, (1999). Soybean Meal - The "Gold Standard". The Farmer's Pride, KPPA News, 11 (20). [Accessed January 18, 2014]. Available online at:

http://www.uky.edu/Ag/AnimalSciences/pubs/soybeanmea l-thegolfstandard.PDF

FAO, (1995). World livestock production systems: Current status, issues and trends. Animal Production and Health Paper N° 127, Food and Agricultre Organization for the United

Nations (FAO). Rome, Italy.

FAO, (1999). Cumbre Mundial sobre la Alimentación. Depósito de documentos de la FAO [in line]. June 1999. [Accessed December 22, 2013]. Available online at: http://www.fao.org/docrep/x2051s/x2051s00.HTM

FAO, (2002). Reducing Poverty and Hunger, the Critical Role of Financing for Food, Agriculture, and Rural Development. World Food Program, Food and Agricultre Organization for the United Nations (FAO). Rome, Italy.

FAO, (2006a). Livestock a major threat to environment. FAONewsroom, Food and Agricultre Organization for the United Nations [in line]. November 2006. [Accessed December 28, 2013]. Available online at: http://www.fao.org/newsroom/en/News/2006/1000448/index.ht ml

FAO, (2006b). World agriculture: towards 2030/2050. Food and Agricultre Organization for the United Nations. Rome, Italy.

FAO, (2009a). 1.02 billion people hungry. News of the Food and Agriculture Organization of the United Nations [in line]. June 2009. [Accessed July 25, 2014]. Available online at: http://www.fao.org/news/story/en/item/20568/icode/

FAO, (2009b). Livestock in the balance. State of Food and Agriculture 2009. Food and Agricultre Organization for the United Nations (FAO). Rome, Italy.

FAO, (2011). Global food losses and food waste – Exent, causes and prevention. Food and Agriculture Organization of the United Nations. Rome, Italy.

FAO, (2012a). The State of Food Insecurity in the World

2012. Food and Agriculture Organization of the United Nations. Rome, Italy.

FAO, (2012b). Top production Soybean 2012 - Food and Agricultural commodities production. FAOSTATS. [Accessed July 25, 2014]. Available online at:

http://faostat.fao.org/site/339/default.aspx

FAO, (2013). Milk Production. Dairy production and products, Food and Agriculture Organization for the United Nations (FAO). Rome, Italy.

FAO, (2014). Food Outlook: Biannual Report on Global Food Markets, May 2014. Trade and Markets Division, Food and Agricultre Organization for the United Nations (FAO). Rome, Italy.

Friedl B, Hammer M, Jager J, Lorek S, Omann I, Pack A, (2007). Sustainable Food Consumption: Trends and Opportunities, Final Report. Sustainable Europe Research Institute (SERI) & Wegener Center for Climate and Global Change. [Accessed March 23, 2014]. Available online at:

http://seri.at/wp-content/uploads/2009/08/final_report_sufotrop_year_2007.pdf

Global Forest Coalition, (2013). Industrial Livestock Production Key Threat to World's Forests and Biodiversity. Global Forest Coalition [in line]. May 2013. [Accessed December 28, 2013]. Available online at:

http://globalforestcoalition.org/2684-industrial-livestock-product ion-key-threat-to-worlds-forests-and-biodiversity

Gómez GR, (2008). Enciclopedia bovina. Facultad de Medicina Veterinaria y Zootecnia, Universidad Autónoma de México. Ciudad de México, México. Online version available at:

http://www.fmvz.unam.mx/fmvz/e_bovina/1AlimentaciondeBovi
nos.pdf

Gustavsson J, Cederberg C, Sonesson U, van Otterdijk R,
Meybeck A, (2011). Global Food Looses and Food Waste. Food
and Agricultre Organization for the United Nations (FAO).
Rome, Italy.

Hurt D, (2012). Beyond the capitalism – Looking to the
future. The Zeitgeist Movement Official Blog [in line]. May
2012. [Accessed December 22, 2013]. Available online at:
http://blog.thezeitgeistmovement.com/blog/daniel-hurt/beyond-c
apitalism-looking-future

Institute of Medicine, (2002). Dietary Reference Intakes
for Energy, Carbohydrate, Fiber, Fat, Fatty Acids, Cholesterol,
Protein, and Amino Acids. Washington (DC): The National
Academies Press; 2002.

INTA, (2009). La soja sigue siendo muy rentable.
Agroinfloclima [in line]. April 2009. [Accessed December 26,
2013]. Available online at: http://agro.infoclima.com/?p=52

INTA, (2011). Como rinden los cultivares de avena y
raigrás. INTAinforma [in line]. February 2011. [Accessed
Decemver 26, 2013]. Available online at:
http://intainforma.inta.gov.ar/?p=4536

INTA, (2012a). Para el INTA, el maíz argentino tiene un
potencial inmejorable. INTAinforma [in line]. September 2012.
[Accessed December 26, 2013]. Available online at:
http://intainforma.inta.gov.ar/?p=13119

INTA, (2013). El rendimiento del trigo crece cada año.
Diario El Tiempo [in line]. April 2013. [Accessed December 26,
2013]. Available online at:

http://www.diarioeltiempo.com.ar/index.php/agropecuarias/174 92-el-rendimiento-del-trigo-crece-cada-ano

Lewis AJ, Southern LL, (2001). Swine nutrition. 2nd edition. CRC Pres.

McIntyre BD, Herren HR, Wakhungu J, Watson R, (2009). International Assessment of Agricultural Knowledge, Science and Technology for Development: Global Report. Island Press, Washington D.C.

Oil World, (2010). Major meals, World summary balances. Oil World Weekly 55(3): 45.

Pimentel D, Pimental M, (2003). Sustainability of meat-based and plant-based diets and the environment. Am J Clin Nutr 78(3): 660-663.

RAE. Definición de economía. Real Academia Española [in line]. Available online at: http://lema.rae.es/drae/srv/search? id=GnPvZSuVpDXX2A2elEUW

Rasby R, (2013). Determining How Much Forage a Beef Cow Consumes Each Day. Institut of Agriculture and Natural Resources (IANE), University of Nebraska-Lincoln [in line]. April 2013. [Accessed December 26, 2013]. Available online at: http://beef.unl.edu/web/cattleproduction/forageconsumed-day

Royal Society. (2009). Reaping the benefits: science and the sustainable intensification of global agriculture. RS Policy Document 11/09. London, UK.

Rudela TK, Schneider L, Uriarte M, Turner BL, DeFries R, Lawrence D, Geoghegan J, Hecht S, Ickowitz A, Lambin EF, Birkenholtz T, Baptista S, Grau R, (2009). Agricultural intensification and changes in cultivated areas, 1970-2005. Proc

Natl Acad Sci USA 106(49): 20675-20680.

Sadava D, Orians GH, (2000). Life: The Science of Biology. New York: W. H. Freeman and Co, 2000: 887.

Steinfeld H, Gerber P, Wassenaar T, Castel V, Rosales M, de Haan C, (2006). Livestock's Long Shadow: Environmental issues and options. FAO/LEAD, Rome, Italy.

SoyTech, (2014). Soy Facts. [Accessed July 25, 2014] Available online at: http://www.soyatech.com/soy_facts.htm

TGOS, (2011). The future of food and farming. Final Project Report. The Government Office for Science (TGOS). London, UK.

The Development Fund, (2010). A viable food future. The Development Fund. Oslo, Norway.

Thornton P, Herrero M, Ericksen P, (2011). Livestock and climate change. Livestock Exchange, International Livestock Research Institute (ILRI); 3. Nairobi, Kenya.

UN, (2000). Resolution 55/2 adopted by the General Assembly: United Nations Millennium Declaration. General Assembly of the United Nations.

UNCCD, (2012). Worsening Factors. United Nations Convention to Combat Desertification [in line]. 2012. [Accessed December 23, 2013]. Available online at: http://www.unccd.int/en/programmes/Thematic-Priorities/Food-Sec/Pages/Wors-Fact.aspx

UNDP, (2014). The Millennium Development Goals. United Nations Development Programme [in line]. 2014. [Accessed July 25, 2014]. Available online at: http://www.undp.org/content/undp/en/home/mdgoverview.html

UNEP, (2011). Towards a green economy: pathways to

sustainabledevelopment and poverty eradication. United Nations Environment Programme (UNEP). Nairobi, Kenya.

UNEP, (2012). Avoiding Famines in the Future: Strengthening the Ecological Basis of Food Security through Sustainable Food Systems. United Nations Environment Programme. Available online at:
http://www.unep.org/publications/ebooks/avoidingfamines/

UNICEF, (2011). Levels and Trends in Child Mortality. Estimates Developed by the UN Interagency Group for Child Mortality Estimation. United Nations International Children's Emergency Fund (UNICEF). New York, USA.

UNICEF, (2012). Prevalencia y tendencias de la desnutrición crónica entre niños pre-escolares, Salud y Nutrición Pública. United Nations International Children's Emergency Fund (UNICEF). New York, USA.

USDA, (2013). Food Availability (Per Capita) Data System. Economic Research Service, United States Deparment of Agriculture (USDA) [in line]. December 2013. [Accessed December 28, 2013]. Available online at:
http://www.ers.usda.gov/data-products/food-availability-(per-cap ita)-data-system.aspx#.Ur7xzY6zDgV

USDA, (2013). World Agricultural Supply and Demand Estimates - 524. United States Department of Agriculture (USDA). Washington D.C, USA.

Viera-Gallo JA, (1977). La crisis mundial de alimentos y el tercer mundo. Nueva Sociedad 29: 30-36.

World Bank. (2007). World Development Report 2008: Agriculture for Development. The World Bank. Washington D.C., USA.

WFP, (2014). Hunger Statistics. World Food Programme – FAO [in line]. 2014. [Accessed July 25, 2014]. Available online at: http://www.wfp.org/hunger/stats

WWF/ZSL/GFN. (2010). Living planet report 2010: biodiversity, biocapacity and development. World Wildlife Fund/Zoological Society of London/Global Footprint Network. Gland, Switzerland.

## Chapter 3: "Environment"

Baillie JEM, Hilton-Taylor C, Stuart SN, (2004). 2004 IUCN Red List of Threatened Species. A Global Species Assessment. International Union for Conservation of Nature (IUCN). Gland, Switzerland and Cambridge, UK.

Butzer KW, (2012). Collapse, environment, and society. Proc Natl Acad Sci USA 109(10): 3632-3639.

Capper JL, (2011). The environmental impact of beef production in the United States: 1977 compared with 2007. J Anim Sci 89: 4249-4261.

Contestabile M, (2012). Failed protection regimes. Nature Climate Change 2: 839.

FAO, (2006). Cattle ranching and deforestation. Livestock policy brief 03. Sector Analysis and Policy Branch (AGAL) of the Animal Production and Health Division of the Food and Agriculture Organization of the United Nations (FAO). Rome, Italy.

FAO, (2013). Livestock's role in deforestation. Livestock, Environment and Development (LEAD), Food and Agriculture

Organization of the United Nations (FAO) [in line]. 2013. [Accessed December 28, 2013]. Available online at: http://www.fao.org/agriculture/lead/themes0/deforestation/en

IUCN, (2013). Summary statistics for globally threatened species. International Union for Conservation of Nature and Natural Resources [in line]. [Accessed December 14, 2013]. Available online at: http://www.iucnredlist.org/about/summary-statistics

MEA, (2005). Current State & Trends Assessment – Chapter 4: Biodiversity. Millennium Ecosystem Assessment (MEA). Washington D.C., USA.

Nguyen, TLT, Hermansen JE, Mogensen L, (2010). Environmental consequences of different beef production systems in the EU. Journal of Cleaner Production 18: 756-766.

Scientific American, (2011). How Does Meat in the Diet Take an Environmental Toll?. Earth Talk, Scientific American Magazine [in line]. December 2011. [Accessed December 28, 2013]. Available online at: http://www.scientificamerican.com/article.cfmid=meat-and-envi ronment

Steinfeld H, Gerber P, Wassenaar T, Castel V, Rosales M, de Haan C, (2006). Livestock's Long Shadow: Environmental issues and options. FAO/LEAD, Rome, Italy.

Subak S, (1999). Global environmental costs of beef production. Ecological Economics 30: 79-91.

UNEP, (2010). Assessing the Environmental Impacts of Consumption and Production: Priority Products and Materials, A Report of the Working Group on the Environmental Impacts of Products and Materials to the International Panel for

Sustainable Resource Management. United Nations Environment Programme (UNEP). Paris, France.

Wilson EO, (1989). Threats to biodiversity. Sci Am 1989, 261: 108-117.


*Deforestation*

Alexandratos N, Bruinsma J, (2012). World Agriculture Towards 2030/2050: The 2012 Revision. Agricultural Development Economics Division (ADED), Food and Agriculture Organization for the United Nations (FAO). Rome, Italy.

Asner GP, Elmore AJ, Olander LP, Martin RE, Harris AT, (2004). Grazyng systems, ecosystem responses and global change. Annu Rev Environ Resour 29: 261-299 .

Barchuk A, Barri F, Britos AH, Cabido M, Fernández J, Tamburini D, (2010). Diagnóstico y perspectivas de los bosques en Córdoba. Revista Hoy la Universidad 4: 52-73.

Boletta PE, Ravelo AC, Planchuelo AM, Grilli M, (2006). Assessing deforestation in the Argentine Chaco. Forest Ecology and Management 228(1-3): 108-114.

Bowman MS, Soares-Filho BS, Merry FD, Nepstad DC, Rodrigues M, Almeida OT, (2012). Persistence of cattle ranching in the Brazilian Amazon: a spatial analysis of the rationale for beef production. Land Use Policy 29: 558-568.

Britos AH, Barchuk AH, (2008). Cambios en la cobertura y en el uso de la tierra en dos sitios del Chaco Árido del noroeste de Córdoba, Argentina. Agriscientia 25(2): 97-110.

Brown S, Zarin D, (2013). What Does Zero Deforestation Mean? Science 342(6160): 805-807.

NRC, (2013). Forest carbon. Natural Resoruces Canada, Government of Canada [in line]. December 2013. [Accessed December 29, 2013]. Available online at: https://www.nrcan.gc.ca/forests/climate-change/13085

Brown T, (1997). Clearances and Clearings: Deforestation in Mesolithic/Neolithic Britain. Oxford Journal of Archaeology 16(2): 133.

Cabido M, Zak MR, (2010). Deforestación, Agricultura y Biodiversidad. Hoy La Univesidad [in line]. June 2010. [Accessed January 8, 2014]. Available online at: http://www.hoylauniversidad.unc.edu.ar/2010/junio/deforestacio n-agricultura-y-biodiversidad-apuntes

Cabido M, Zak MR, Cingolani A, Cáceres DM, Díaz S. Cambios en la cobertura de la vegetación del centro de Argentina. ¿Factores directos o causas subyacentes?. En: Oesterheld M, Aguiar MR, Ghersa C, Paruelo JM. "La heterogeneidad de la vegetación de los agroecosistemas". Editorial Facultad de Agronomía. Buenos Aires, Argentina. 2005. p. 273-302.

Callahan C, (2001). Rainforest Deforestation. Rainforest Alliance [in line]. May 2001. [Accessed December 29, 2013]. Available online at: http://kanat.jsc.vsc.edu/student/callahan/mainpage.htm

Cederberg C, Meyer D, Flysjö A, (2009). Life cycle inventory of greenhouse gas emissions and use of land and energy in Brazilian beef production. Swedish Institute of Food and Biotechnology (SIK). Göteborg, Sweden.

CIFOR, (2012). Forest and Water. Factsheets No 6. Center for International Forestry Research (CIFOR). Bogor,

Indonesia.

Clark G, (1947). Forest clearance and prehistoric farming. Economic History Review 17(1): 45-51.

Delgado C, Rosegrant M, Meijer S, (2001). Livestock to 2020: The Revolution Continues. Paper presented at the annual meetings of the International Agricultural Trade Research Consortium (IATRC), Auckland, New Zealand.

EPI, (2013). Food and Agriculture. Earth Policy Institute (EPI) [in line]. December 2013. [Accessed December 31, 2013]. Available online at:
http://www.earthpolicy.org/data_center/C24

FAO, (2009). The State of Food and Agriculture. Food and Agricultre Organization for the United Nations. Rome, Italy.

FAO, (2012). States of the World's Forest. Food and Agriculture Organization of the United Nations. Rome, Italy.

FAO, (2013). Forest and Water: International Momentum and Action. Food and Agriculture Organization of the United Nations (FAO), Rome, Italy.

FAO, (2014). Food Outlook: Biannual Report on Global Food Markets, May 2014. Trade and Markets Division, Food and Agricultre Organization for the United Nations. Rome, Italy.

Fearnside PM, (2005). Deforestation in Brazilian Amazonia: History, Rates and Consequences. Conservation Biology 19: 680-688 .

FRA, (2010). Global Forest Resources Assessment 2010. Food and Agriculture Organization of the United Nations. Rome, Italy.

Füher E, (2000). Forest functions, ecosystem stability and management. Forest Ecology and Management 2000; 132(1):

29-38.

Galloway JN, Burke M, Bradford GE, Naylor R, Falcon W, Chapagain AK, Gasell JC, McMullough E, Mooney HA, Olsen KL, Steinfeld H, Wassenaar T, Smil V, (2007). International trade in meat: The tip of the pork chop. Ambio 36(8): 622–629.

GB Historical GIS, (2009). A Vision of Britain through Time. England through time, University of Portsmouth [in line]. 2009. [Accessed December 29, 2013]. Available online at: http://www.visionofbritain.org.uk/unit/10061325/cube/TOT_POP

GEO, (2004). Perspectivas del Medio Ambiente para la Argentina. Programa de las Naciones Unidas para el Medio Ambiente (PNUMA) y Secretaría de Ambiente y Desarrollo Sustentable (SAyDS), Ministerio de Salud y Ambiente de la Nación. Buenos Aires, Argentina.

Gibbs HK, Ruesch AS, Achard F, Clayton MK, Holmgren P, Ramankutty N, Foley JA, (2010). Tropical forests were the primary sources of new agricultural land in the 1980s and 1990s. Proc Nat Acad Sci 107(38): 16732-16737.

Greenpeace, (2006). Devorando el Amazonia. Greenpeace Internacional. Amsterdam, Holanda.

Nepstad DC, Stickler CM, Soares- Filho B, Merry F, (2008). Interactions among Amazon land use, forests and climate: prospects for a near-term forest tipping point. Philos Trans R Soc Lond B Biol Sci 363(1498): 1737-1746.

Greenpeace, (2009). Amazon Cattle footprint, Mato Grosso: State of Destruction. Greenpeace Brazil. Sao Paul, Brazil.

Hansen MC, Potapov PV, Moore R, Hancher M,

Turubanova SA, Tyukavina A, Thau D, Stehman SV, Goetz SJ, Loveland TR, Kommareddy A, Egorov A, Chini L, Justice CO, Townshend RG, (2013). High-Resolution Global Maps of 21st-Century Forest Cover Change. Science 342(6160): 850-853.

Homer JB, Sloan AP, (1982). Theories of the Industrial Revolution: A Feedback Perspective. Dinamica 1982; 8, Part I Summer.

INDEC, (1988–2002). Censo Nacional Agropecuario. Provincia Santiago del Estero. Instituto Nacional de Estadısticas y Censos (INDEC), Secretarıa de Planificacion, Presidencia de la Nacion, Republica Argentina.

InfoLeg, (2007). Ley Nacional 26.331 de "Presupuestos Mínimos de Protección Ambiental de los Bosques Nativos". Información Legislativa (InfoLeg), Centro de Documentación e Información (CDI), Ministerio de Economía y Finanzas Públicas (MECON). Buenos Aires, Argentina.

Goldewijk CGM, Battjes JJ, (1997). HYDE, version 1.1. National Institute of Public Health and the Environment (RIVM). Bilthoven, Netherlands.

Kreis S, (2001). The Origins of the Industrial Revolution in England, Lecture 17. The History Guide [in line]. Agoust 2011. [Accessed December 29, 2013]. Available online at: http://www.historyguide.org/intellect/lecture17a.html

Maarten Dros J, (2004). Managing the soy boom: Two scenarios of soy production expansion in South America. AIDEnvironment. Amsterdam, Neatherlands.

Margulis S, (2004). Causes of Deforestation of the Brazilian Amazon; Working paper no 22. World Bank.

Washington D.C., United States.

May PH, Millikan B, Gebara MF, (2010). The context of REDD+ in Brazil: Drivers, agents, and institutions. Center for International Forestry Research (CIFOR). Bogor, Indonesia.

Merenson C, (2011). ¿Agricultura sostenible o Síndrome "Pamphúmedo"?. Los Verdes Blog [in line]. September 2011. [Accessed January 4, 2014]. Available online at: http://losverdes.org.ar/blog/?p=623

Moglia G, Gimenez AM, (1998). Rasgos anatómicos característicos del hidrosistema de las principales especies arbóreas de la región chaqueña argentina. Investigación Agraria: Sistemas y Recursos Forestales 7: 53-71.

Morello J, Mateucci SD, (2000). Singularidades territoriales y problemas ambientales de un país asimétrico y terminal. Realidad Económica [in line]. January 2000. [Accessed January 4, 2014]. Available online at: http://www.iade.org.ar/modules/noticias/article.php?storyid=648

Morin J, (2008). Brazilian Ministry of Agriculture's Ten-Year Projections; GAIN report BR8636. USDA Foreign Agricultural Service. Washington D.C., USA.

Morton DC, DeFries RS, Shimabukuro YE, Anderson LO, Arai E, del Bon Espirito-Santo F, Freitas R, Morisette J, (2006). Cropland expansion changes deforestation dynamics in the southern Brazilian Amazon. Proc Nat Acad Sci 103(39): 14637-14641.

Nierenberg D, (2003). Meat Production and Consumption Grow. Vital Signs 2003: 30-32.

PEA, (2013). Plan Estratégico Agroalimentario y

Agroindustrial. Ministerio de Agricultura, Ganadería y Pesca. Presidencia de la Nación. Buenos Aires, Argentina.

SFA, (2008). Deforestation. The Dictionary of Forestry, Society of American Foresters [in line]. July 2008. [Accessed December 29, 2014]. Available online at: http://dictionaryofforestry.org/dict/term/deforestation

Soares-Filho BS, Nepstad DC, Curran LM, Cerqueira GC, Garcia RA, Ramos CA, Voll E, McDonald A, Lefebvre P, Schlesinger P, (2006). Modelling conservation in the Amazon basin. Nature 440: 520-523.

Speedy AW, (2003). Global Production and Consumption of Animal Source Foods. J Nutr 133(11): 4048-4053.

Swift MJ, Andren O, Brussaard L, Briones M, Couteaux MM, Ekschmitt K, Kjoller A, Loiseau P, Smith P, (1998). Global change, soil biodiversity, and nitrogen cycling in terrestrial ecosystems: three case studies. Global Change Biology 4(7): 729-743.

TNC/FVSA/DeSdel Chaco/WCS, (2005). Evaluación Ecorregional del Gran Chaco Americano. The Nature Conservancy (TNC), Fundación Vida Silvestre Argentina (FVSA), Fundación para el Desarrollo Sustentable del Chaco (DeSdel Chaco) y Wildife Conservation Society Bolivia (WCS). Fundación Vida Silvestre Argentina. Buenos Aires, Argentina.

UMSEF, (2007). Primer Inventario Nacional de Bosques Nativos. Unidad de Manejo del Sistema de Evaluación Forestal (UMSEF), Dirección de Bosques de la Nación, Secretaria de Ambiente y Desarrollo Sostenible. Buenos Aires, Argentina.

UMSEF, (2012). Monitoreo de la Superficie de Bosque Nativo de la República Argentina : Período 2006-2011. Unidad de Manejo del Sistema de Evaluación Forestal (UMSEF), Dirección de Bosques de la Nación, Secretaria de Ambiente y Desarrollo Sostenible. Buenos Aires, Argentina.

UN, (1999). The World at Six Billions. Population Division. United Nations (UN). New York, USA.

UNCC, (2013). REDD+ and Desertification. Thematic Factsheets series No.7. United Nations Convention to Combat Desertification (UNCC). Bonn, Germany.

Viano L, (2013). Uno de los peores desmontes en 4 años. Ciudadanos, La Voz del Interior [in line]. February 2014. [Accessed February 9, 2014]. Available online at: http://www.lavoz.com.ar/ciudadanos/uno-de-los-peores-desmontes-en-4-anos

Wassenaar T, Gerber P, Verburg PH, Rosales M, Ibrahim M, Steinfeld H, (2007). Projecting land use changes in the Neotropics: The geography of pasture expansion into forest. Glob Env Change 17: 86-104.

Williams M, (2000). Dark ages and dark areas: global deforestation in the deep past. Journal of Historical Geography 28-46.

Williams M, (2002). Deforesting the earth: from prehistory to global crisis. Chicago, USA, University of Chicago Press.

World Meters, (2013). World Population: Past, Present and Future [in line]. 2013. [Accessed December 29, 2013]. Available online at: http://www.worldometers.info/world-population/#pastfuture

WWF/ZSL/GFN, (2010). Living planet report 2010: biodiversity, biocapacity and development. World Wildlife

Fund/Zoological Society of London/Global Footprint Network. Gland, Switzerland.

Zak MR, Cabido M, Hodgson JG, (2004). Do subtropical seasonal forests in the Gran Chaco, Argentina, have a future? Biological Conservation 120: 589-598.

*Water usage*

Allan JA, (1993). Fortunately there are substitutes for water otherwise our hydro-political futures would be impossible. Priorities for water resources allocation and management, ODA, London, pp. 13-26.

Arienza M, Carsen Pittaluga AE, Gómez MA, Marschoff CM, (2011). Agua: Panorama general en la Argentina. Green Cross Argentina. Buenos Aires, Argentina.

Arnell NW, (2004). Climate change and global water resources: SRES emissions and socio-economic scenarios. Glob Environ Chang 14(1): 31-52.

Ercin AE, Hoekstra AY, (2014). Water footprint scenarios for 2050: A global analysis. Environ Int 64: 71-82.

Falkenmark M, Molden D, (2008). Wake up to realities of river basin closure. International Journal of Water Resources Development 24: 201-215.

FAO, (1997). Water Resources of the Near-East Region: a Review. Food and Agriculture of the United Nations (FAO). Rome, Italy.

FAO, (2011). The state of the world's land and water resources for food and agriculture (SOLAW) – Managing systems at risk. Food and Agriculture Organization of the United Nations (FAO). Rome, Italy and Earthscan, London, UK.

Frenken K, Gillet V, (2012). Irrigation water requirement and water withdrawal by country. AQUASTATS, Land and Water Division, Food and Agriculture Organization of the United Nations (FAO). Rome, Italy.

Fung F, Lopez A, New M, (2011). Water availability in +2 °C and +4 °C worlds. Philos Trans R Soc Lond A 369(1934): 99-116.

Gerten D, Schaphoffa S, Haberlandtb U, Luchta W, Sitch S, (2004). Terrestrial vegetation and water balance: hydrological evaluation of a dynamic global vegetation model. Journal of Hydrology 286: 249-270.

Hoekstra AY, (2003). Virtual Water: An introduction. Value of Water Research Report Series No. 12, Proceedings of the International Expert Meeting on Virtual Water Trade. Delft, Netherlands.

Hoekstra AY, Chapagain AK, Aldaya MM, Mekonnen MM. The water footprint assessment manual: Setting the global standard. London, UK and Washington D.C., USA: Earthscan. 2011.

Hoekstra, AY, Hung PQ, (2002). Virtual water trade: A quantification of virtual water flows between nations in relation to international crop trade. Value of Water Research Report Series No.11, IHE, Delft, Netherlands.

Hutson SS, Barber NL, Kenny JF, Linsey KS, Lumia DS, Maupin MA, (2004). Estimated use of water in the United States in 2000. US Geological Survey Circular 1268, p. 46.

IWMI, (2007). Water for Food, Water for Life: A Comprehensive Assessment of Water Management in Agriculture. London: Earthscan and Colombo: International

Water Management Institute.

IWMI/SIWI, (2005). Water – More nutrition per drop. International Water Management Institute (IWMI) and the Stockholm International Water Institute (SIWI). Stockholm, Sweden.

Mekonnen MM, Hoekstra AY, (2012). A global assessment of the water footprint of farm animal products. Ecosystems 15(3): 401-415.

Milly PCD, Dunne KA, Vecchia AV, (2005). Global pattern of trends in streamflow and water availability in a changing climate. Nature 438(7066): 347-350.

Nuwer R, (2011). Not All Rivers Reach the Sea. The New York Times [in line]. November 2011. [Accessed January 11, 2014]. Available online at:
http://green.blogs.nytimes.com/2011/11/17/all-rivers-do-not-run-to-the-sea/?_php=true&_type=blogs&_r=0

OECD, (2012). Environmental outlook to 2050: The Consequences of Inaction. Highlights. Organization for Economic Co-operation and Development (OECD).

Renault D, Wallender WW, (2000). Nutritional Water Productivity and Diets. Agricultural Water Management 45: 275-296.

SIWI, (2012). Feeding a Thirsty World – Challenges and Opportunities for a Water and Food Secure Future. Report Nr. 31. Stockholm International Water Institute (S IWI). Stockholm, Sweden.

Unión Europea, (2011). El agua es la vida: La directiva marco sobre aguas contribuye a proteger los recursos de Europa. Unión Europea. Bélgica.

USGS, (2013).The water cycle. United States Geological Survey, U.S. Department of the Interior [in line]. November 2013. [Accessed January 12, 2014]. Available online at: http://ga.water.usgs.gov/edu/watercycle.html

Vanham D, Hoekstra AY, Bidoglio G, (2013). Potential water saving through changes in European diets. Environ Int 61: 45-56.

WWAP, (2012). The United Nations World Water Development Report 4: Managing Water under Uncertainty and Risk. World Water Assessment Programme (WWAP), UNESCO. Paris, France.

### *Water pollution and watershed degradation*

Barrow CJ, (1998). River Basin Development Planning and Management: A Critical Review. World Development 26(1): 171-186.

Belsky AJ, Blumenthal DM, (1997). Effects of Livestock Grazing on Stand Dynamics and Soils in Upland Forests of the Interior West. Conservation Biology 11(2): 315–327.

Belsky AJ, Matzke A, Uselman S, (1999). Survey of livestock influences on stream and riparian ecosystems in the western United States. Journal of Soil and Water Conservation 54: 419-431 .

Brauman KA, Daily GC, Duarte TK, Mooney HA, (2007). The Nature and Value of Ecosystem Services: An Overview Highlighting Hydrologic Services. Annu Rev Environ Resour 32: 67-98.

Cabido M, Antón A, Cabrera M, Cingolani A, Di Tada I, Enrico L, Funes G, Haro G, Polop J, Renison D, Rodríguez V,

Roqué Garzón J, Rosacher C, Zak M, (2003). Línea de base y programa de monitoreo de la biodiversidad del Parque Nacional Quebrada del Condorito y la Reserva Hídrica Provincial Pampa de Achala. Administración de Parques Nacionales. Córdoba, Argentina.

CDC, (2013). Antibiotic resistance threats in the United States, 2013. Center for Dissease Control and Prevention, U.S. Department of Health and Human Services. Washington DC, USA.

Chagas CI, Morettón J, Santanatoglia OJ, Paz M, Muzio H, De Servi M, Castiglioni M, (2006). Indicadores de contaminación biológica asociados a la erosión hídrica en una cuenca de Pampa Ondulada, Argentina. Cienc suelo 24 (1).

Chislock MF, Doster E, Zitomer RA, Wilson AE, (2013). Eutrophication: Causes, Consequences, and Controls in Aquatic Ecosystems. Nature Education Knowledge 4(4): 10

Cingolani AM, Cabido M, Renison D, Solís-Neffa V, (2003). Combined effects of environment and grazing on vegetation structure in Argentine granite grasslands. Journal of Vegetation Science 14: 223-232.

Cingolani AM, Falczuck V, (2003). Elaboración de un plan de manejo integrado del Parque Nacional Quebrada del Condorito y la Reserva Hídrica Provincial de Achala. 4o Informe de Consultoría. Administración de Parques Nacionales. Córdoba, Argentina.

Cingolani AM, Noy-Meir I, Renison D, Cabido M, (2008). La ganadería extensiva, ¿es compatible con la conservación de la biodiversidad y de los suelos? Ecología Austral 18: 253-271.

Diaz JR, Rosenberg R, (2008). Spreading Dead Zones and

Consequences for Marine Ecosystems. Science 321: 926.

EPA, (2004). Risk Assessment Evaluation for Concentrated Animal Feeding Operations. National Risk Management Research Laboratory (NRMRL), U.S. Environmental Protection Agency (EPA). Cincinnati, United States.

GBA, (2009). Decreto reglamentario de la ley 5965, ecología efluentes gaseosos: reglamentación. Generadores de emisiones gaseosas-medioambiente-atmosfera; y Decreto reglamentario de la ley 5965, protección a las fuentes de provisión y a los cursos y cuerpos receptores de agua y a la atmósfera. Gobierno de Buenos Aires, Argentina. Pp: 2.

Gerber P, Menzi H, (2006). Nitrogen losses from intensive livestock farming systems in Southeast Asia: A review of current trends and mitigation options. International Congress Series 1293: 253-261.

Giorgis MA, Cingolani AM, Teich I, Renison D, Hensen I, (2010). Do Polylepis australis trees tolerate herbivory? Seasonal patterns of shoot growth and its consumption by livestock. Plant Ecol 207: 307-319.

Gorse JE, Steeds DR, (1987). Desertification in the Sahelian and Sudanian zones in West Africa. World Bank technical paper; no WTP 61. Washington DC, USA: The World Bank.

Heil L, (2013). Comunidades de Aves de las Sierras Grandes de Córdoba. Erosión, fragmentación y heterogeneidad: Incidencia antrópico-ambiental (Tesis doctoral). Universidad Nacional de Córdoba, Argentina.

Hudson TD, (2008). Livestock Management and Water

Quality. Washington States University Extension and U.S. Department of Agriculture. Washington DC, United States.

INA, (2004). Inundaciones repentinas en las Sierras de Córdoba. Primeras Jornadas de debate sobre riesgo hídrico, inundaciones y catástrofes. Instituto Nacional de Agua (INA), Instituto Argentino de Recursos Hídrico (IARH), Centro Argentino de Ingenieros (CAI). Buenos Aires, Argentina.

Jameson J, Ramsay PM, (2007). Changes in high-altitude Polylepis forest cover and quality in the Cordillera de Vilcanota, Peru, 1956-2005. Biological Conservation 138: 38-46.

Lunt ID, Eldridge DI, Morgan JW, Bradd Witt G, (2007). A framework to predict the effects of livestock grazing and grazing exclusion on conservation values in natural ecosistems in Australia. Aust J Bot 55: 401-415.

Marcora PI, Renison D, País-Bosch AI, Cabido MR, Tecco PA, (2013). The effect of altitude and grazing on seedling establishment of woody species in central Argentina. Forest Ecology and Management 291: 300-307.

Marshall BM, Levy SB, (2011). Food Animals and Antimicrobials: Impacts on Human Health. Clin Microbiol Rev 24(4): 718-733.

Mwendera EJ, Saleem MAM, Dibabe A, (1997). The effect of livestock grazing on surface runoff and soil erosion from sloping pasture lands in the Ethiopian highlands. Aust J Exp Agr 37: 421- 430.

NOAA, (2011). NOAA-supported scientists find large dead zone in Gulf of Mexico. NOAA News (National Oceanic and Atmospheric Administration) [in line]. Agosto 2011. [Accessed January 14, 2014]. Available online at:

http://www.noaanews.noaa.gov/stories2011/20110804_deadzon e.html

Nosetti L, Herrero MA, Pol M, Maldonado May V, Iramain S, Flores M, (2002). Cuantificación y caracterización de agua y efluentes en establecimientos lecheros, parte I. Demanda de agua y manejo de fluentes. Revista Investigación Veterinaria (INVET FCVet. UBA) 4(1): 7-43.

NRDC, (2013a). Facts about Pollution from Livestock Farms. Natural Resource Defense Council [in line]. February 2013. [Accessed January 13, 2014]. Available online at: http://www.nrdc.org/water/pollution/ffarms.asp

NRDC, (2013b). Pollution from Giant Livestock Farms Threatens Public Health. Natural Resource Defense Council [in line]. February 2013. [Accessed January 13, 2014]. Available online at:

http://www.nrdc.org/water/pollution/nspills.asp

NYT, (1995). Huge Spill of Hog Waste Fuels an Old Debate in North Carolina. The New Yor Times [in line]. June 1995. [Accessed January 13, 2014]. Available online at:

http://www.nytimes.com/1995/06/25/us/huge-spill-of-hog-waste-f uels-an-old-debate-in-north-carolina.html

Palacio RG, Bisigato AJ, Bouza PJ, (2014). Soil erosion in three grazed plant comminities in northeastern Patagonia. Land Degrad Dev doi:10.1002/ldr.2289.

Pinos-Rodríguez JM, García-López JC, Peña-Avelino Y, Rendón-Huerta JA, González-González C, Tristán-Patiño F, (2012). Impactos y regulaciones ambientales del estiércol generado por los sistemas ganaderos de algunos países de América. Agrociencia 46: 359-370.

Renison D, Cingolani AM, (1998). Experiencias en germinación y reproducción vegetativa aplicadas a la reforestación con Polylepis australis (Rosaceae) en las Sierras Grandes de Córdoba, Argentina. Agriscientia 15: 47-53.

Renison D, Hensen I, Cingolani AM, (2004). Anthropogenic soil degradation affects seed viability in Polylepis australis mountain forests of Central Argentina. Forest Ecology and Management 196: 327-333.

Renison D, Hensen I, Suarez R, Cingolani A, (2006). Cover and growth habit of Polylepis woodlands and shrublands in the mountains of Central Argentina: human or environmental influence? J Biogeogr 33: 876-887.

Robledo G, Urcelay C, Rajchenberg M, (2003). New species causing decay on living Polylepis australis in Córdoba, central Argentina. Mycologia 95(2): 347-353.

Sardia GM, Floresb M, Herreroa MA, (2012). Percepción ambiental de productores agropecuarios y docentes rurales del partido de Arrecifes, Buenos Aires, Argentina. AUGMDOMUS 4: 25-41.

Science, (2013). FDA Moves to Reduce Antibiotics in Livestock. Science News [in line]. December 2013. [Accessed January 14, 2014]. Available online at:
http://news.sciencemag.org/health/2013/12/fda-moves-reduce-antibiotics-livestock

SJR, (2011). Illinois hog farm will pay fines over manure spill. The State Jorunal Register [in line]. December 2011. [Accessed January 13, 2014]. Available online at
http://www.sj-r.com/x2105828791/Illinois-hog-farm-will-pay-fines-over-manure-spill

Suarez ML, Renison D, Marcora PI, Hensen I, (2008). Age–size–habitat relationships for Polylepis australis: dealing with endangered forest ecosystems. Biodivers Conser 17: 2617-2625.

Sullivan C, ClimateWire, (2013). Can Livestock Grazing Stop Desertification?. Scientific American [in line]. March 2013. [Accessed January 17, 2014]. Available online at: http://www.scientificamerican.com/article.cfm?id=can-livestock-grazing-stop-desertification

USFWS, (2009). Impacts of Grazing. National Wildlife Refuge System, U.S. Fissh & Wildlife Service [in line]. February 2009. [Accessed January 17, 2014]. Available online at: http://www.fws.gov/invasives/stafftrainingmodule/methods/grazing/impacts.html

### Global Warming and Climatic Change

Barclay JMG, (2012). Meat, a damaging extravagence: a response to Grumett and Gorringe. The Expository Times 123(2): 70-73.

BBC, (2010). Q&A: Professor Phil Jones. BBC [in line]. February 2010. [Accessed February 21, 2014]. Available online at: http://news.bbc.co.uk/2/hi/8511670.stm

Black R, (2010). UN body to look at meat and climate link. BBC [in line]. March 2010. [Accessed February 21, 2014]. Available online at: http://news.bbc.co.uk/2/hi/science/nature/8583308.stm

Carlsson-Kanyama A, Gonzalez A, (2009). Potential contributions of food consumption patterns to climate change.

Am J Clin Nutr 89(suppl): 1704S–179S.

Chang S, (2009). UCLA goes green. Los Angeles Times [in line]. April 2009. [Accessed February 21, 2014]. Available online at: http://latimesblogs.latimes.com/greenspace/2009/04/ucla-takes-collective-green-action-.html

Cook J, (2010). The Scientific Guide to Global Warming Skepticism. Skeptical Science [in line]. December 2010. [Accessed February 20,2014]. Available online at: http://www.skepticalscience.com/docs/Guide_to_Skepticism.pdf

Cook J, Nuccitelli D, Green SA, Richardson M, Winkler B, Painting R, Way R, Jacobs P, Skuce A, (2013). Quantifying the consensus on anthropogenic global warming in the scientific literature. Environ Res Lett 8: 024024.

EPA, (2014). Overview of Greenhouse Gases. United States Environmental Protection Agency [in line]. January 2014. [Accessed February 21, 2014]. Available online at: http://www.epa.gov/climatechange/ghgemissions/gases.html

Fiala, N. (2008). Meeting the Demand: An Estimation of Potential Future Greenhouse Gas Emissions from Meat Production. Ecological Economics 67: 412-419.

Gerber PJ, Steinfeld H, Henderson B, Mottet A, Opio C, Dijkman J, Falcucci A, Tempio G, (2013). Tackling climate change through livestock – A global assessment of emissions and mitigation opportunities. Food and Agriculture Organization of the United Nations (FAO). Rome, Italy.

Gill M, Smith P, Wilkinson JM, (2010). Mitigating climate change: the role of domestic livestock. Animal 4: 323-333.

Hansen J, Fung I, Lacis A, Rind D, Lebedeff S, Ruedy R,

Russell G, Stone P, (1988). Global climate changes as forecast by Goddard Institute for Space Studies three-dimensional model. J Geophys Res 93: 9341-9364.

Hansen J, Sato M, Ruedy R, Lo K, Lea DW, Medina-Elizade M, (2006). Global temperature change. Proc Natl Acad Sci USA 103: 14288-14293.

Hedenus F, Wirsenius S, Johansson DJA, (2014). The importance of reduced meat and dairy consumption for meeting stringent climate change targets. Climatic Change 124:79-91.

IPCC, (2007). Climate Change 2007: The Physical Science Basis. Contribution of Working Group I to the Fourth Assessment Report of the Intergovernmental Panel on Climate Change. Cambridge University Press, Cambridge, UK and New York, USA.

IPCC, (2013). Climate Change 2013: The Physical Science Basis. Contribution of Working Group I to the Fifth Assessment Report of the Intergovernmental Panel on Climate Change. Cambridge University Press, Cambridge, UK and New York, USA.

JSAS, (2010). Joint science academies' statement: Global response to climate change. [Accessed February 21, 2014]. Available online at:
http://nationalacademies.org/onpi/06072005.pdf

NASA. Climate change: How do we know? National Aeronautics and Space Administration [in line]. [Accessed February 20, 2014]. Available online at:
http://climate.nasa.gov/evidence

Nellemann C, MacDevette M, Manders T, Eickhout B, Svihus B, Prins AG, Kaltenborn BP, (2009). The environmental food crisis – The environment's role in averting future food crises. A UNEP rapid response assessment. United Nations Environment Programme, GRID-Arendal. Norway.

NOAA. Global Warming. National Oceanic and Atmospheric Administration [in line]. [Accessed February 21, 2014]. Available online at:
http://www.ncdc.noaa.gov/monitoring-references/faq/global-war ming.php

Pitesky ME, Stackhouse KR, Mitloehner FM, (2009). Clearing the air: Livestock's contribution to climate change. Advances in Agronomy, 103: 2-40.

Place SE, Mitloehner FM, (2012). Beef production in balance: Considerations for life cycle analyses . Meat Science 92: 179-181.

Rahmstorf S, Cazenave A, Church JA, Hansen JE, Keeling RF, Parker DE, Somerville RCJ, (2007).    Recent Climate Observations Compared to Projections. Science 316(5825): 709.

SAIC, (2006). Life Cycle Assessment: Principles and Practice. Scientific Applications International Corporation, National Risk Management Research Laboratory, U.S. Enviromental Protection Agency. Ohio, USA.

Scarborough P, Appleby PN, Mizdrak A, Briggs ADM, Travis RC, Bradbury KE, Key TJ, (2014). Dietary greenhouse gas emissions of meat-eaters, fish-eaters, vegetarians and vegans in the UK. Climatic Change 125(2): 179-192.

Schurer AP, Tett SFB, Hegerl GC, (2014). Small influence of solar variability on climate over the past millennium. Nature Geoscience 7: 104-108.

Society of Chemical Industry, (2008). "Burpless" Grass

Cuts Methane Gas From Cattle, May Help Reduce Global Warming. ScienceDaily [in line]. May 2008. [Accessed February 21, 2014]. Available online at:

www.sciencedaily.com/releases/2008/05/080506120859.htm

Stocker TF, (2013). The closing door of climate targets. Science 339(6117): 280-282.

UNEP, (2013). The Emissions Gap Report 2013. United Nations Environment Programme (UNEP). Nairobi, Kenya.

Stackhouse-Lawson KR, Rotz CA, Oltjen JW, Mitloehner FM, (2012). Carbon footprint and ammonia emissions of California beef production systems. J Anim Sci 90(12): 4641-4655.

UNFCC, (1992). United Nations Framework Convention on Climate Change. United Nations (UN). New York, USA.

WCRP, (2012). Atmosphere, Oceans and Climate. World Climate Research Programme [in line]. December 2012. [Accessed February 20, 2014]. Available online at: http://www.wcrp-climate.org/oceanclim.shtml

Williams DR, (2013). Earth Fact Sheet. National Space Science Data Center [in line]. July 2013. [Accessed February 20, 2014]. Available online at:

http://nssdc.gsfc.nasa.gov/planetary/factsheet/earthfact.html

WMO, (2013). The global climate 2001–2010: A decade of climate extremes. Sumary Report. World Meteorological Organization (WMO). Geneve, Switzerland.

World Bank, (2012). Turn down the heat. Why a 4 °C warmer world must be avoided. A report for the World Bank by the Potsdam Institute for Climate Impact Research and Climate Analytics. Washington, D.C., USA.

## Chapter 3: "Health"

AAP, (2013). Vegetarian diets for children. American Academy of Pediatrics [in line]. Agoust 2013. [Accessed February 10, 2014]. Available online at:
http://www.healthychildren.org/English/ages-stages/gradeschool/nutrition/pages/Vegetartian-Diet-for-Children.aspx

ACS, (2010). Vegetarianism. American Cancer Society [in line]. May 2010. [Accessed February 10, 2014]. Available online at:
http://www.cancer.org/treatment/treatmentsandsideeffects/complementaryandalternativemedicine/dietandnutrition/vegetarianism

AEDN, (2009). Postura de la Asociación Americana de Dietética: Dietas Vegetarianas. Asociación Española de Dietistas-Nutricionistas [in line]. November 2009. [Accessed February 9, 2014]. Available online at:
http://www.grep-aedn.es/documentos/vegetariandiets.pdf

AHA, (2013). Vegetarian Diets. American Hearth Association [in line]. January 2013. [Accessed February 13, 2014]. Available online at:
http://www.heart.org/HEARTORG/GettingHealthy/NutritionCenter/Vegetarian-Diets_UCM_306032_Article.jsp

Albert MJ, Mathan VI, Baker SJ, (1980). Vitamin B12 synthesis by human small intestinal bacteria. Nature 283(5749): 781-782.

Allen RH, Stabler SP, (2008). Identification and

quantitation of cobalamin and cobalamin analogues in human feces. Am J Clin Nutr 87(5):1324-35.

Amit M, (2010). Vegetarian diets in children and adolescents. Paediatr Child Health 15(5): 303-308.

Appel LJ, (2009). ASH position paper: dietary approaches to lower blood pressure. J Am Soc Hypertens 3(5): 321-331.

Appel LJ, Moore TJ, Obarzanek E, Vollmer WM, Svetkey LP, Sacks FM, Bray GA, Vogt TM, Cutler JA, Windhauser MM, Lin PH, Karanja N, (1997). A clinical trial of the effects of dietary patterns on blood pressure. DASH Collaborative Research Group. N Engl J Med 336: 1117-1124.

Appleby PN, Allen NE, Key TJ, (2011). Diet, vegetarianism, and cataract risk. Am J Clin Nutr 93(5): 1128-1135.

Appleby PN, Davey GK, Key TJ, (2002). Hypertension and blood pressure among meat eaters, fish eaters, vegetarians and vegans in EPIC-Oxford, Public Health Nutr 5: 645-654.

Aslinia F, Mazza JJ, Yale SH, (2006). Megaloblastic Anemia and Other Causes of Macrocytosis. Clin Med Res 4(3): 236-241.

Aune D, Ursin G, Veierod MB, (2009). Meat consumption and the risk of type 2 diabetes: a systematic review and meta-analysis of cohort studies. Diabetologia 52: 2277-2287.

Barnard ND, Cohen J, Jenkins DJ, Turner-McGrievy G, Gloede L, Jaster B, Seidl K, Green AA, Talpers S, (2006) A low-fat vegan diet improves glycemic control and cardiovascular risk factors in a randomized clinical trial in individuals with type 2 diabetes. Diabetes Care 29: 1777-1783.

Barnard ND, Katcher HI, Jenkins DJ, Cohen J,

Turner-McGrievy G, (2009). Vegetarian and vegan diets in type 2 diabetes management. Nutr Rev 67(5): 255-263.

Barrett JF, Whittaker PG, Williams JG, Lind T, (1994). Absorption of non-haem iron from food during normal pregnancy. BMJ 309: 79-82 .

Beeson WL, Mills, PK, Phillips RL, Andress M, Fraser GE, (1989). Chronic disease among Seventh-day Adventists, a low-risk group. Cancer 64: 570-581.

Ben Q, Sun Y, Chai R, Qian A, Xu B, Yuan Y, (2013). Dietary Fiber Intake Reduces Risk for Colorectal Adenoma: A Meta-Analysis. Gastroenterology pii: S0016-5085(13) 01586-2.

Berkow SE, Barnard N, (2006). Vegetarian diets and weight status. Nutr Rev 64(4): 175-88.

Berkow SE, Barnard ND, (2005). Blood pressure regulation and vegetarian diets. Nutr Rev 63: 1-8.

Bernstein AM, Treyzon L, Li Z, (2007). Are high-protein, vegetable-based diets safe for kidney function? A review of the literature. J Am Diet Assoc 107(4): 644-650.

Bradley P, (2012). Diet composition and obesity. The Lancer 379(9821): 1100.

Burkert NT, Muckenhuber J, GroBschädl F, Rásky É, Freidl W, (2014). Nutrition and Health – The Association between Eating Behavior and Various Health Parameters: A Matched Sample Study. PLoS ONE 9(2): e88278.

Burr ML, Butland BK, (1988). Heart disease in British vegetarians. Am J Clin Nutr 48(3 suppl): 830-832.

Chang-Claude J, Hermann S, Eilber U, Steindorf K, (2005). Lifestyle determinants and mortality in German vegetarians and health-conscious persons: results of a 21-year follow-up. Cancer Epidemiol Biomarkers Prev 14: 963-968.

Choi HK, Atkinson K, Karlson EW, Willett W, Curhan G, (2004). Purine-rich foods, dairy and protein intake, and the risk of gout in men. N Engl J Med 350: 1093-1103.

Cook JD, (1996). Adaptation in iron metabolism. Am J Clin Nutr 51: 301-308.

Craig WJ, Mangels AR, (2009). Position of the American Dietetic Association: vegetarian diets. J Am Diet Assoc 109(7): 1266-1282.

Cross AJ, Leitzmann MF, Gail MH, Hollenbeck AR, Schatzkin A, Sinha R, (2007). A prospective study of red and processed meat intake in relation to cancer risk. PloS Med 4: e325.

Davey GK, Spencer EA, Appleby PN, Allen NE, Knox KH, Key TJ, (2003). EPIC-Oxford: lifestyle characteristics and nutrient intakes in a cohort of 33883 meat-eaters and 31546 non meat-eaters in the UK. Public Health Nutr 6: 259-269.

Day L, (2013). Proteins from land plants - Potential resources for human nutrition and food security. Trends in Food Science & Technology 32: 25-42.

De Biase SG, Fernandes SF, Gianini RJ, Duarte JL, (2007). Vegetarian diet and cholesterol and triglycerides levels. Arq Bras Cardiol 88: 35-39.

de Mello VD, Zelmanovitz T, Perassolo MS, Azevedo MJ, Gross JL, (2006). Withdrawal of red meat from the usual diet reduces albuminuria and improves serum fatty acid profile in type 2 diabetes patients with macroalbuminuria. Am J Clin Nutr 83: 1032-1038.

De Pergola G, Silvestris F, (2013). Obesity as a Major Risk

Factor for Cancer. J Obes 2013: 291546.

Demetriou D, (2013). Japanese cuisine gets UNESCO heritage status. The Telegraph [in line]. December 2013. [Accessed February 9, 2014]. Available online at: http://www.telegraph.co.uk/news/worldnews/asia/japan/104963 26/Japanese-cuisine-gets-UNESCO-heritage-statusj.html

Dewell A, Weidner G, Sumner MD, Chi CS, Ornish D. A very-low-fat vegan diet increases intake of protective dietary factors and decreases intake of pathogenic dietary factors. J Am Diet Assoc 108: 347-356.

Dietitians of Canada, (2013). Vegetarian Diets. Dietitians of Canada [in line]. 2013. [Accessed February 9, 2014]. Available online at: http://www.dietitians.ca/Your-Health/Nutrition-A-Z/Vegetarian-D iets.aspx

Dwyer JT, Mayer LD, Kandel RF, Mayer J, (1973). The new vegetarians. J Am Diet Assoc 62: 503-509.

Elkan AC, Sjöberg B, Kolsrud B, Ringertz B, Hafström I, Frostegård J, (2010). Gluten-free vegan diet induces decreased LDL and oxidized LDL levels and raised atheroprotective natural antibodies against phosphorylcholine in patients with rheumatoid arthritis: a randomized study. Arthritis Res Ther 10: R34.

Fardet A, (2010). New hypotheses for the health protective mechanisms of whole-grain cereals: what is beyond fibre? Nutr Res Rev 23: 65-134.

Farmer B, Larson BT, Fulgoni VL 3rd, Rainville AJ, Liepa GU, (2011). A vegetarian dietary pattern as a nutrient-dense approach to weight management: an analysis of the national health and nutrition examination survey 1999-2004. J Am Diet Assoc 111(6): 819-827.

Ferrante D, Linetzky B, Konfino J, King A, Virgolini M, Laspiur S, (2011). Encuesta nacional de factores de riesgo 2009: Evolución de la epidemia de enfermedades crónicas no transmisibles en Argentina. Estudio de corte transversal. Rev Argent Salud Pública 2(6): 34-41.

Ferrante D, Virgolini M, (2007). Encuesta Nacional de Factores de Riesgo 2005: resultados principales. Prevalencia de factores de riesgo de enfermedades cardiovasculares en la Argentina. Rev Arg Cardiol 75(1): 20-2.

Flegal KM, Kit BK, Orpana H, Graubard BI, (2013). Association of all-cause mortality with overweight and obesity using standard body mass index categories: a systematic review and meta-analysis. JAMA 309(1): 71-82.

Fletcher J, Frisvold D, Tefft N, (2013). Substitution Patterns Can Limit the Effects of Sugar Sweetened Beverage Taxes on Obesity. Prev Chronic Dis 0:120195.

Fontoira L, (2013). Historia del asado argentino. Diario Democracia [in line]. April 2013. [Accessed February 9, 2014]. Available online at: http://www.diariodemocracia.com/notas/2013/4/6/historia-asado -argentino-55298.asp

Fraser GE, (1999). Associations between diet and cancer, ischemic heart disease, and all cause mortality in non-Hispanic white California Seventh-day Adventists. Am J Clin Nutr 70(3 suppl): 532S-538S.

Fraser GE, (2009). Vegetarian diets: what do we know of their effects on common chronic diseases? Am J Clin Nutr 89(5):

1607S-1612S.

Fung TT, Schulze M, Manson JE, Willett WC, Hu FB, (2004). Dietary patterns, meat intake, and the risk of type 2 diabetes in women. Arch Intern Med 164: 2235-2240.

Gaesser GA, (2007). Carbohydrate quantity and quality in relation to body mass index. J Am Diet Assoc 107: 1768-1780.

Garcia G, Sunil TS, Hinojosa P, (2012). The Fast Food and Obesity Link: Consumption Patterns and Severity of Obesity. Obes Surg 22: 810-818.

Garton L, (2011). Vegetarian diets - Keeping a healthy balance. The British Dietetic Association [in line]. Agoust 2011. [Accessed February 9, 2014]. Available online at: http://www.bda.uk.com/foodfacts/vegetarianfoodfacts.pdf

Genkinger JM, Koushik A, (2007). Meat Consumption and Cancer Risk. PLoS Med 4(12): e345.

Gilsing AM, Crowe FL, Lloyd-Wright Z, Appleby PN, Allen NE, Key TJ, (2010). Serum concentrations of vitamin B12 and folate in British male omnivores, vegetarians and vegans: results from a cross-sectional analysis of the EPIC-Oxford cohort study. Eur J Clin Nutr 64: 933-939.

Gofrit ON, Shemer J, Leibovici D, Modan B, Shapira SC, (2000). Quaternary prevention: a new look at an old challenge. Isr Med Assoc J 2: 498-500.

González-Vallinas M, González-Castejón M, Rodríguez-Casado A, Ramírez de Molina A, (2013). Dietary phytochemicals in cancer prevention and therapy: a complementary approach with promising perspectives. Nutr Rev 71(9): 585-599.

Gullett NP, Ruhul Amin AR, Bayraktar S, (2010). Cancer

prevention with natural compounds. Semin Oncol 37: 258-281.

Haddad EH, Berk LS, Kettering JD, Hubbard RW, Peters WR, (1999). Dietary intake and biochemical, hematologic and immune status of vegans compared with nonvegetarians. Am J Clin Nutr 70(3): 586-593.

Hallberg L, (1981). Bioavailability of dietary iron in man. Annu Rev Nutr 1: 123-147.

Hardinge MG, Crooks H, (1963). Non-flesh dietaries, II: scientific literature. J Am Diet Assoc 43: 550-558.

Hardinge MG, Crooks H, Stare FJ, (1962). Nutritional studies of vegetarians: IV. Dietary fatty acids and serum cholesterol levels. Am J Clin Nutr 10: 516-54.

Hardinge MG, Stare FJ, (1954a). Nutritional studies of vegetarians: I. Nutritional, physical, and laboratory studies. J Clin Nutr 2: 73-82.

Hardinge MG, Stare FJ, (1954b). Nutritional studies of vegetarians: II. Dietary and serum levels of cholesterol. J Clin Nutr 2: 83-8.

Havala S, Dwyer J, (1993). Position of the American Dietetic Association: vegetarian diets. J Am Diet Assoc 93(11): 1317-1319.

Hensrud DD, (2000). Clinical Preventive Medicine in Primary Care: Background and Practice: 1. Rationale and Current Preventive Practices. Mayo Clinic Proceedings 75(2): 165-172.

Herrmann W, Schorr H, Purschwitz K, Rassoul F, Richter V, (2001). Total homocysteine, vitamin B12 and total antioxidant status in vegetarians Clin Chem 47: 1094-1101.

Hong S, Cai Q, Chen D, Zhu W, Huang W, Li Z, (2012).

239

Abdominal obesity and the risk of colorectal adenoma: a meta-analysis of observational studies. Eur J Cancer Prev 21(6): 523-531.

Huang T, Yang B, Zheng J, Li G, Wahlqvist ML, Li D, (2012). Cardiovascular disease mortality and cancer incidence in vegetarians: a meta-analysis and systematic review. Ann Nutr Metab 60(4): 233-240.

Humes DJ, West J, (2011). Diet and risk of diverticular disease. BMJ 343: d4115.

Hunt JR, (2003). Bioavailability of iron, zinc, and other trace minerals from vegetarian diets. Am J Clin Nutr 78(3): 633S-639S.

Hunt JR, Roughead ZK, (2000). Adaptation of iron absorption in men consuming diets with high or low iron bioavailability. Am J Clin Nutr 71: 94-102.

Jiang R, Manson JE, Meigs JB, Ma J, Rifai N, Hu FB, (2004). Body iron stores in relation to risk of type 2 diabetes in apparently healthy women. JAMA 291: 711-717.

Key T, Davey G, (1996). Prevalence of obesity is low in people who do not eat meat. BMJ 313: 816-817 (letter).

Key TJ, Appleby PN, Spencer EA, Travis RC, Roddam AW, Allen NE, (2009). Mortality in British vegetarians: results from the European Prospective Investigation into Cancer and Nutrition (EPIC-Oxford). Am J Clin Nutr 89: 1613S-1619S.

Key TJ, Fraser GE, Thorogood M, Appleby PN, Beral V, Reeves G, Burr ML, Chang-Claude J, Frentzel-Beyme R, Kuzma JW, Mann J, McPherson K, (1999). Mortality in vegetarians and nonvegetarians: Detailed findings from a collaborative analysis of 5 prospective studies. Am J Clin Nutr 70(suppl): 516S-524S.

Kuhn TS, (1962). The structure of scientific revolutions. Chicago: University of Chicago Press.

Lagiou P, Talamini R, Samoli E, Lagiou A, Ahrens W, Pohlabeln H, Benhamou S, Bouchardy C, Slamova A, Schejbalova M, Merletti F, Richiardi L, Kjaerheim K, Agudo A, Castellsague X, Macfarlane TV, Macfarlane GJ, Biggs AM, Barzan L, Canova C, Simonato L, Lowry RJ, Conway DI, McKinney PA, Znaor A, McCartan BE, Healy CM, Marron M, Hashibe M, Brennan P, (2009). Diet and upper-aerodigestive tract cancer in Europe: the ARCAGE study. Int J Cancer 124: 2671-2676.

Lam TK, Cross AJ, Consonni D, Randi G, Bagnardi V, Bertazzi PA, Caporaso NE, Sinha R, Subar AF, Landi MT, (2009). Intakes of red meat, processed meat, and meat mutagens increase lung cancer risk. Cancer Res 69: 932-939.

Law MR, Wald NJ, Wu T, (1994). Systematic underestimation of association between serum cholesterol concentration and ischaemic heart disease in observational studies: data from the BUPA study. BMJ 308: 363-366.

Liu RH, (2013). Dietary bioactive compounds and their health implications. J Food Sci 78 Suppl 1: A18-25.

Luan de C, Li H, Li SJ, Zhao Z, Li X, Liu ZM, (2008). Body iron stores and dietary iron intake in relation to diabetes in adults in north China. Diabetes Care 31: 285-286.

MacLean WC, Graham GG, (1980). Vegetarianism in children. Am J Dis Child 134: 513-519.

Manach C, Scalbert A, Morand C, Rémésy C, Jiménez L, (2004). Polyphenols: food sources and bioavailability. Am J Clin Nutr 79(5): 727-747.

Margetts BM, Beilin LJ, Vandongen R, Armstrong BK, (1986). Vegetarian diet in mild hypertension: a randomised controlled trial. Br Med J (Clin Res Ed) 293: 1468-1471.

Martínez JA, Cordero P, Campión J, Milagro FI, (2012). Interplay of early-life nutritional programming on obesity, inflammation and epigenetic outcomes. Proc Nutr Soc 71(2): 276-83.

Mattes RD, (2008). The energetics of nut consumption. Asia Pac J Clin Nutr 17(1): 337-339.

Messina VK, Burke KI, (1997). Position of the American Dietetic Association: vegetarian diets. J Am Diet Assoc 11: 1317-1321.

Micha R, Michas G, Mozaffarian D, (2012). Unprocessed Red and Processed Meats and Risk of Coronary Artery Disease and Type 2 Diabetes – An Updated Review of the Evidence. Curr Atheroscler Rep 14(6): 515-524.

MinSN, (2006). Primera Encuesta Nacional de Factores de Riesgo. Informe de resultados. Ministerio de Salud de la Nación. Primera edición. Buenos Aires. ISBN 950-38-0039-0 [Accessed January 14, 2014]. Available online at: http://msal.gov.ar/htm/site/enfr/resultados.asp

Moe SM, Zidehsarai MP, Chambers MA, Jackman LA, Radcliffe JS, Trevino LL, Donahue SE, Asplin JR, (2011). Vegetarian Compared with Meat Dietary Protein Source and Phosphorus Homeostasis in Chronic Kidney Disease. Clin J Am Soc Nephrol 6(2): 257-264.

Nair P, Mayberry JF, (1994). Vegetarianism, dietary fibre and gastro-intestinal disease. Dig Dis 12: 177-185.

NHS, (2012). Cardiovascular disease – Risk factors.

Nathional Health Service [in line]. July 2012. [Accessed February 14, 2014]. Available online at: http://www.nhs.uk/Conditions/cardiovascular-disease/Pages/Risk-factors.aspx

NIH, (2013a). Protein in diet. U.S. National Library of Medicine, National Institutes of Health [in line]. April 2013. [Accessed July 21, 2014]. Available onlie at: http://www.nlm.nih.gov/medlineplus/ency/article/002467.htm

NIH, (2013b). Iron in diet. U.S. National Library of Medicine, National Institutes of Health [in line]. February 2013. [Accessed July 21, 2014]. Available onlie at: http://www.nlm.nih.gov/medlineplus/ency/article/002422.htm

O'Keefe SJ, (2008). Nutrition and colonic health: the critical role of the microbiota. Curr Opin Gastroenterol 24(1): 51-58.

Obersby D, Chappell DC, Dunnett A, Tsiami AA, (2013). Plasma total homocysteine status of vegetarians compared with omnivores: a systematic review and meta-analysis. Br J Nutr 109(5): 785-794.

Orlich MJ, Singh PN, Sabaté J, Jaceldo-Siegl K, Fan J, Knutsen S, Beeson WL, Fraser GE, (2013). Vegetarian dietary patterns and mortality in Adventist Health Study 2. JAMA Intern Med 173(13): 1230-1238.

Pan A, Sun Q, Bernstein AM, Schulze MB, Manson JE, Stampfer MJ, Willett WC, Hu FB, (2012). Red Meat Consumption and Mortality: Results from Two Prospective Cohort Studies. Arch Intern Med 172(7): 555-563.

Pawlak R, Lester SE, Babatunde T, (2014). The prevalence of cobalamin deficiency among vegetarians assessed by serum vitamin B12: a review of literature. Eur J Clin Nutr 68(5): 541-548.

Pawlak R, Parrott SJ, Raj S, Cullum-Dugan D, Lucus D, (2013). How prevalent is vitamin B(12) deficiency among vegetarians? Nutr Rev 71(2): 110-117.

Petterson BJ, Anousheh R, Fan J, Jaceldo-Siegl K, Fraser GE, (2011). Vegetarian diets and blood pressure among white subjects: results from the Adventist Health Study-2 (AHS-2). Pub Health Nutr 15(10): 1909-1916.

Phillips RL, Garfinkel L, Kuzma JW, Beeson WL, Lotz T, Brin B, (1980). Mortality among California Seventh-day Adventists for selected cancer sites. J Natl Cancer Inst 65: 1097-1107.

Phillips RL, Lemon FR, Beeson WL, Kuzma JW, (1978). Coronary heart disease mortality among Seventh-Day Adventists with differing dietary habits: a preliminary report. Am J Clin Nutr 31: S191-S198.

Pixley F, Wilson D, McPherson K, Mann J. Effect of vegetarianism on development of gall stones in women. Br Med J (Clin Res Ed) 291: 11-12.

Priyadarsini RV, Nagini S, (2012). Cancer chemoprevention by dietary phytochemicals: promises and pitfalls. Curr Pharm Biotechnol 13(1): 125-136.

Rand WM, Pellet PL, Young VR, (2003). Meta-analysis of nitrogen balance studies for estimating protein requirements in healthy adults. Am J Clin Nutr 77(1): 109-127.

Rao V, Al-Weshahy A, (2008). A plant-based diets and

control of lipids and coronary heart disease risk. Curr Atheroscler Rep 10: 478.

Reddy MB, (2005). Algorithms to assess non-heme iron bioavailability. Int J Vitam Nutr Res 75: 405-412.

Register UD, Sonnenbeg LM, (1973). The vegetarian diet. J Am Diet Assoc 62: 253-61.

Reilly JJ, Kelly J, (2011). Long-term impact of overweight and obesity in childhood and adolescence on morbidity and premature mortality in adulthood: systematic review. Int J Obes (Lond) 35(7): 891-898.

Rohrmann S, Overvad K, Bueno-de-Mesquita HB, Jakobsen MU, Egeberg R, Tjønneland A, Nailler L, Boutron-Ruault M, Clavel-Chapelon F, Krogh V, Palli D, Panico S, Tumino R, Ricceri F, Bergmann MM, Boeing H, Li K, Kaaks R, Khaw K, Wareham NJ, Crowe FL, Key TJ, Naska A, Trichopoulou A, Trichopoulos D, Leenders M, Peeters PHM, Engeset D, Parr CL, Skeie G, Jakszyn P, Sánchez MJ, Huerta JM, Redondo ML, Barricarte A, Amiano P, Drake I, Sonestedt E, Hallmans G, Johansson I, Fedirko V, Romieux I, Ferrari P, Norat T, Vergnaud AC, Riboli E, Linseisen J, (2013). Meat consumption and mortality - results from the European Prospective Investigation into Cancer and Nutrition. BMC Med 11: 63.

Rosell M, Appleby P, Spencer E, Key T, (2006). Weight gain over 5 years in 21,966 meat-eating, fish-eating, vegetarian, and vegan men and women in EPIC-Oxford. Int J Obes (Lond) 30(9): 1389-1396.

Rouse IL, Beilin LJ, Armstrong BK, Vandongen R, (1983). Blood-pressure-lowering effect of a vegetarian diet: controlled trial in normotensive subjects. Lancet 1: 5-10.

Rouse IL, Beilin LJ, Mahoney DP, Margetts BM, Armstrong BK, Record SJ, Vandongen R, Barden A, (1986). Nutrient intake, blood pressure, serum and urinary prostaglandins and serum thromboxane B2 in a controlled trial with a lacto-ovo-vegetarian diet. J Hypertens 4: 241-250.

Sabaté J, (2003). The contribution of vegetarian diets to health and disease: a paradigm shift?. Am J Clin Nutr 78(3): 502-507.

Sabaté J, Duk A, Lee CL, (1999). Publication trends of vegetarian nutrition articles in biomedical literature, 1966–1995. Am J Clin Nutr 70(3): 601-607.

Sabaté J, Wien M, (2010). Vegetarian diets and childhood obesity prevention. Am J Clin Nutr 91(5): 1525S-1529S.

Salleras L, (1994). La medicina clínica preventiva: el futuro de la prevención. Med Clin (Barc) 102(1): 5-12.

Sanders TA, (2009). DHA status of vegetarians. Prostaglandins Leukot Essent Fatty Acids 81: 137-141.

Schatzkin A, Park Y, Leitzmann MF, Hollenbeck AR, Cross AJ, (2008). Prospective study of dietary fiber, whole grain foods, and small intestinal cancer. Gastroenterology 135: 1163-1167.

Schulze MB, Manson JE, Willett WC, Hu FB, (2003). Processed meat intake and incidence of type 2 diabetes in younger and middle-aged women. Diabetologia 46: 1465-1473.

SCP, (2010). Presidencia de la Nación. Manzur: Un país se hace grande cuando cuida a sus chicos. Se presentó en Córdoba el informe del ProSanE. Sala de Prensa, Secretararía de Comunicación Pública [in line]. November 2010. [Accessed May 15,2013]. Available online at:
http://www.prensa.argentina.ar/2010/11/25/14204-manzur-un-p

ais-se-hace-grande-cuando-cuida-a-sus-chicos.php

Siener R, Hesse A, (2003). The effect of a vegetarian and different omnivorous diets on urinary risk factors for uric acid stone formation. Eur J Nutr 42: 332-337.

Sinha R, Cross AJ, Graubard BI, Leitzmann MF, Schatzkin A, (2009). Meat intake and mortality: a prospective study of over half a million people. Arch Intern Med 169(6): 562-571.

Siriwardhana N, Kalupahana NS, Moustaid-Moussa N, (2012). Health benefits of n-3 polyunsaturated fatty acids: eicosapentaenoic acid and docosahexaenoic acid. Adv Food Nutr Res 65: 211-22.

Sköldstam L, Brudin L, Hagfors L, Johansson G, (2005). Weight reduction is not a major reason for improvement in rheumatoid arthritis from lacto-vegetarian, vegan or Mediterranean diets. Nutr J 4:15.

Smedslund G, Byfuglien MG, Olsen SU, Hagen KB, (2010). Effectiveness and safety of dietary interventions for rheumatoid arthritis: a systematic review of randomized controlled trials. J Am Diet Assoc 110(5): 727-735.

Snowdon DA, Phillips RL, (1985). Does a vegetarian diet reduce the occurrence of diabetes? Am J Public Health 75: 507-512.

Snowdon DA, Phillips RL, (1985). Does a vegetarian diet reduce the occurrence of diabetes? Am J Public Health 75: 507-512.

Snowdon DA, Phillips RL, Fraser GE, (1984). Meat consumption and fatal ischemic heart disease. Prev Med 13: 490-500.

Spencer EA, Appleby PN, Davey GK, Key TJ, (2003). Diet

and body mass index in 38000 EPIC-Oxford meat-eaters, fish-eaters, vegetarians and vegans. Int J Obes Relat Metab Disord 27: 728-734.

Story M, Kaphingst KM, Robinson-O'Brien R, Glanz K, (2008). Creating Healthy Food and Eating Environments: Policy and Environmental Approaches. Annu Rev Public Health 29: 253-272.

Tarleton S, DiBaise JK, (2011). Low-residue diet in diverticular disease: putting an end to a myth. Nutr Clin Pract 26(2): 1337-1342.

Terra, (2003). Asado, empanada y dulce de leche: ¿patrimonio argentino?. Terra [in line]. April 2003. [Accessed February, 2014]. Available online at: http://www.terra.com.ar/canales/informaciongeneral/66/66924.html

Tonstad S, Butler T, Yan R, Fraser GE., (2009). Type of vegetarian diet, body weight, and prevalence of type 2 diabetes. Diabetes Care 32(5): 791-796.

U.S. Department of Agriculture & U.S. Department of Health and Human Services, (2010). Dietary Guidelines for Americans, 2010. 7th Edition, Washington, DC: U.S. Government Printing Office, December 2010.

van Dokkum W, de Boer BC, van Faassen A, Pikaar NA, Hermus RJ, (1983). Diet, faecal pH and colorectal cancer. Br J Cancer 48: 109-110.

Vang A, Singh PN, Lee JW, Haddad EH, Brinegar CH, (2008). Meats, processed meats, obesity, weight gain and occurrence of diabetes among adults: findings from Adventist Health Studies. Ann Nutr Metab 52: 96-104.

Vargas A, Montaño E, (2010). Comida mexicana, patrimonio inmaterial de la humanidad. La Jornada [in line]. November 2010. [Accessed February 9, 2014]. Available online at: http://www.jornada.unam.mx/2010/11/17/index.php?section=politica&article=002n1pol

VíaRestó, (2010). El asado. VíaRestó, Clarín [in line]. April 2010. [Accessed February 9, 2014]. Available online at: http://viaresto.com/Notas/El-asado-660.aspx

Davis BC, Kris-Etherton PM, (2003). Achieving optimal essential fatty acid status in vegetarians: current knowledge and practical implications. Am J Clin Nutr 78(3 suppl): 640S-646S.

Walcher T, Haenle MM, Mason RA, Koenig W, Imhof A, Kratzer W, (2010). The effect of alcohol, tobacco and caffeine consumption and vegetarian diet on gallstone prevalence. Eur J Gastroenterol Hepatol 22(11): 1345-1351.

Wang Y, Beydoun MA, (2009). Meat consumption is associated with obesity and central obesity among US adults. Int J Obes (Lond) 33(6): 621-628.

Watanabe F, (2007). Vitamin B12 sources and bioavailability. Exp Biol Med (Maywood) 232: 1266-1274.

Watanabe F, Takenaka S, Kittaka-Katsura H, Ebara S, Miyamoto E, (2002). Characterization and bioavailability of vitamin B12-compounds from edible algae. J Nutr Sci Vitaminol (Tokyo) 48(5): 325-31.

Welch AA, Shakya-Shrestha S, Lentjes MAH, Wareham NJ, Khaw K-T, (2010). Dietary intake and status of n-3 polyunsaturated fatty acids in a population of fish-eating and non-fish-eating meat-eaters, vegetarians and vegans and the precursor-product ratio of {alpha}-linolenic acid to long-chain n-3 polyunsaturated fatty acids: results from the EPIC-Norfolk cohort. Am J Clin Nutr 92: 1040-1051.

Whittaker PG, Barrett JF, Lind T (2001). The erythrocyte incorporation of absorbed nonhaem iron in pregnant women. Br J Nutr 86: 323-329.

WHO, (2013a). Obesity and Overweight. World Health Organization [in line]. March 2013. [Accessed February 14, 2014]. Available online at:

http://www.who.int/mediacentre/factsheets/fs311/en

WHO, (2013b). The top 10 caues of death. Media centre, World Heatlh Organzation [in line]. July 2013. [Accessed February 14, 2014]. Available online at:

http://who.int/mediacentre/factsheets/fs310/en/

Wyatt SB, Winters KP, Dubbert PM, (2006). Overweight and obesity: prevalence, consequences, and causes of a growing public health problem. Am J Med Sci 331(4): 166-174.

Yashodhara BM, Umakanth S, Pappachan JM, Bhat SK, Kamath R, Choo BH, (2009). Omega-3 fatty acids: a comprehensive review of their role in health and disease. Postgrad Med J 85: 84-90.

Young VR, Pellet PL, (1994). Plant proteins in relation to human protein and amino acid nutrition. Am J Clin Nutr 59: 1203-1212.

Zhang Z, Ma G, Chen S, Li Z, Xia E, Sun Y, Yang F, Zheng L, Feng X, (2013). Comparison of plasma triacylglycerol levels in vegetarians and omnivores: ameta-analysis. Nutrition 29(2): 426-430.

## Chapter 5: "Some myths..."

Armelagos GJ, Goodman AH, Jacobs KH, (1991). The origins of agriculture: Population growth during a period of declining health. Population and Environment 13(1): 9-22.

Bae CJ, (2013). Archaic Homo sapiens. Nature Education Knowledge 4(8): 4.

Berkowitz M, (1996). World's Earliest Wine. Archaelogy (Archive) 49(5).

Biesalski HK, Truswell S, Hill M, (2002). Meat Consumption: Evolution and Progress. European Journal of Clinical Nutrition 56(12): 1270-1278.

Blanco D, (2013). Dieta paleolítica, una tendencia mundial que cada vez suma más adeptos entre los argentinos. Infobae [in line]. September 2013. [Accessed March 5, 2014]. Available online at:
http://www.infobae.com/2013/09/19/1510007-dieta-paleolitica-una-tendencia-mundial-que-cada-vez-suma-mas-adeptos-los-argentinos

Bocquet-Appel J, (2008). Explaining the Neolithic Demographic Transition. The Neolithic Demographic Transition and its Consequences 35-55.

Caspari R, Lee SH, (2004). Older age becomes common late in human evolution. Proc Natl Acad Sci USA 101(30): 10895-10900.

CDC, (2013). State Indicator Report on Fruits and Vegetables 2013. Centers for Disease Control and Prevention

(CDC), U.S. Department of Health and Human Services. Atlanta, USA.

Club Nutriconal, (2011). La Causa Primaria del Cáncer: Alimentos Alcalinos vs. Alimentos Acidificantes. Club Nutricional [in line]. Agoust 2011. [Accessed February 17, 2014]. Available online at:
http://club-nutricional.com/dietas/2011/08/29/causa-primaria-del-cancer/

Constantino PJ, (2013). The "Robust" Australopiths. Nature Education Knowledge 4(1): 1.

Cordain L, Eaton SB, Sebastian A, Mann N, Lindeberg S, Watkins BA, O'Keefe JH, Brand-Miller J, (2005). Origins and evolution of the Western diet: health implications for the 21st century. Am J Clin Nutr 81(2): 341-354.

Crawford MA, (1990). The early development and evolution of the human brain. Ups J Med Sci Suppl 48: 43-78.

Dethlefsen L, McFall-Ngai M, Relman DA, (2007). An ecological and evolutionary perspective on human–microbe mutualism and disease. Nature 449: 811-818

Dorey F, (2013). Homo habilis. Australian Museum [in line]. September 2013. [Accessed February 18, 2014]. Available online at:
http://australianmuseum.net.au/Homo-habilis/

Eiberg H, Troelsen J, Nielsen M, Mikkelsen A, Mengel-From J, Kjaer KW, Hansen L, (2008). Blue eye color in humans may be caused by a perfectly associated founder mutation in a regulatory element located within the HERC2 gene inhibiting OCA2 expression. Hum Genet 123(2): 177-87.

Estebaranz F, Galbany J, Martínez LM, Turbón D,

Pérez-Pérez A, (2012). Buccal dental microwear analyses support greater specialization in consumption of hard foodstuffs for Australopithecus anamensis. Journal of Anthropological Sciences 90: 1-24.

Fenton TR, Lyon AW, Eliasziw M, Tough SC, Hanley DA, (2009). Meta-analysis of the effect of the acid-ash hypothesis of osteoporosis on calcium balance. J Bone Miner Res 24(11): 1835-1840.

Fenton TR, Tough SC, Lyon AW, Eliasziw M, Hanley DA, (2011). Causal assessment of dietary acid load and bone disease: a systematic review & meta-analysis applying Hill's epidemiologic criteria for causality. Nutr J 10: 41.

Fiorenza L, Benazzi S, Jeremy T, Kullmer O, Bromage TG, Schrenk F, (2011). Molar Macrowear Reveals Neanderthal Eco-Geographic Dietary Variation. PLoS ONE 6(3): e14769.

Flatz G, Rotthauwe HW, (1973). Lactose nutrition and natural selection. Lancet 2: 76-77.

WCRF/AICR, (2007). Food, Nutrition, Physical Activity, and the Prevention of Cancer. World Cancer Research Fund and the American Institute for Cancer Research. Washington, D.C.: AICR, 2007.

Furuse Y, Suzuki A, Oshitani H, (2010). Origin of measles virus: Divergence from rinderpest virus between the 11th and 12th centuries. Virology Journal 7: 52.

Gatenby RA, Gillies RJ, (2004). Why do cancers have high aerobic glycolysis? Nature Reviews Cancer 4(11): 891-899.

Guzik S. Investigating the Diet of Neanderthals. Smithsonian Institue, National Museum of Natural History [in line]. [Accessed February 18, 2014]. Available online at:

http://www.mnh.si.edu/highlight/Neanderthal_Diet/

Hancock AM, Witonsky DB, Ehler E, Alkorta-Aranburu G, Beall C, Gebremedhin A, Sukernik R, Utermann G, Pritchard J, Coop G, Di Rienzo A, (2010). Human adaptations to diet, subsistence, and ecoregion are due to subtle shifts in allele frequency. Proc Natl Acad Sci USA 107(2): 8924-8930.

Heaney RP, Rafferty K, (2001). Carbonated beverages and urinary calcium excretion. Am J Clin Nutr 74(3): 343-347.

Helmuth H, (1998). Body height, body mass and surface area of the Neanderthals. Zeitschrift Für Morphologie Und Anthropologie 82 (1): 1-12.

Henry AG, Brooks AS, Piperno DR, (2010). Microfossils in calculus demonstrate consumption of plants and cooked foods in Neanderthal diets (Shanidar III, Iraq; Spy I and II, Belgium). Proc Natl Acad Sci USA 108(2): 486-491.

Henry AG, Ungar PS, Passey BH,Sponheimer M, Rossouw L, Bamford M, Sandberg P, de Ruiter DJ, Berger L, (2012). The diet of Australopithecus sediba. Nature 2012. doi:10.1038/nature11185

Hill K, Hurtado AM, Walker RS, (2006). High adult mortality among Hiwi hunter-gatherers: Implications for human evolution. Journal of Human Evolution 52: 443-454.

HSPH a. Calcium and Milk: What's Best for Your Bones and Health? The Nutrition Source, Harvard School of Public Health [in line]. [Accessed February 18, 2014]. Available online at:
http://www.hsph.harvard.edu/nutritionsource/calcium-full-story/#calcium-from-milk

HSPH b. Food Pyramids and Plates: What Should You

Really Eat? The Nutrition Source, Harvard School of Public Health [in line]. [Accessed February 18, 2014]. Available online at:

http://www.hsph.harvard.edu/nutritionsource/pyramid-full-story/

Itan Y, Powell A, Beaumont MA, Burger J, Thomas MG, (2009). The Origins of Lactase Persistence in Europe. PLoS Comput Biol 5(8): e1000491.

JHM, (2009). Cancer Email Hoax – Spanish Version. Jonh Hopkins Medicine [in line]. April 2009. [Accessed February 17, 2014]. Available online at:

http://www.hopkinsmedicine.org/kimmel_cancer_center/news_e vents/spanish_email_hoax.html

Kim JW, Dang CV, (2006). Cancer's molecular sweet tooth and the Warburg effect. Cancer Res 66 (18): 8927-8930.

Kwiatkowski DP, (2005). How Malaria Has Affected the Human Genome and What Human Genetics Can Teach Us about Malaria. Am J Hum Genet 77(2): 171-192.

Leonard WR, (2002). Food for Thought Dietary change was a driving force in human evolution. Scientific American [in line]. December 2002. [Accessed March 5, 2014]. Available online at:

http://www.freerepublic.com/focus/news/791969/posts

Leonard WR, Snodgrass JJ, Robertson ML, (2010). Evolutionary Perspectives on Fat Ingestion and Metabolism in Humans. In: Montmayeur JP, le Coutre J, editors. Fat Detection: Taste, Texture, and Post Ingestive Effects. Boca Raton (FL): CRC Press; 2010. Chapter 1. Available online at: http://www.ncbi.nlm.nih.gov/books/NBK53561/

Leonardia M, Gerbaultb P, Thomasb MG, Burger J, (2012)

.The evolution of lactase persistence in Europe. A synthesis of archaeological and genetic evidence. International Dairy Journal 22(2): 88-97 .

Ley RE, Lozupone CA, Hamady M, Knight R, Gordon JI, (2008). Worlds within worlds: evolution of the vertebrate gut microbiota. Nat Rev Microbiol 6(10): 776-788.

Lindeberg S, Cordain L, Eaton SB, (2003). Biological and Clinical Potential of a Palaeolithic Diet. Journal of Nutritional and Environmental Medicine 13(3): 149-160.

Magill CR, Ashley GM, Freeman KH, (2013a). Ecosystem variability and early human habitats in eastern Africa. Proc Natl Acad Sci USA 110: 1167-1174.

Magill CR, Ashley GM, Freeman KH, (2013b). Water, plants, and early human habitats in eastern Africa. Proc Natl Acad Sci USA 110: 1175-1180.

Marcott SA, Shakun JD, Clark PU, Mix AC, (2013). A Reconstruction of Regional and Global Temperature for the Past 11,300 Years. Science 339(6124): 1198-1201.

Mayo Clinic, (2013). Risk factors – Osteoporosis. Mayo Clinic [in line]. July 2013. [Accessed February 17, 2014]. Available online at:
http://www.mayoclinic.org/diseases-conditions/osteoporosis/basics/risk-factors/CON-20019924

McArdle J, (1991). Humans are Omnivores. Vegetarian Journal (The Vegetarian Resource Group) [in line]. [Accessed February 18, 2014]. Available online:
http://www.vrg.org/nutshell/omni.htm

Moore GE, (1903). Principia Ethica. Cambridge: Cambridge University Press. ISBN 0-334-04040-X.

National Geographic. Omnivore. Education, National Geographic Society [in line]. [Accessed February 18, 2014]. Available online at: http://education.nationalgeographic.com/education/encyclopedia/omnivore/?ar_a=4&ar_r=3

NIH, (2012). Lactose intolerancia. U. S. National Library of Medicine [in line]. October 2012. [Accessed March 5, 2014]. Available online: http://www.nlm.nih.gov/medlineplus/ency/article/000276.htm

Nikander R, Sievänen H, Heinonen A, Daly RM, Uusi-Rasi K, Kannus P, (2010). Targeted exercise against osteoporosis: A systematic review and meta-analysis for optimising bone strength throughout life. BMC Med 8: 47.

Remer T, Friedrich M, (1995). Potential Renal Acid Load of Foods and its Influence on Urine pH. J Am Diet Assoc 95: 791-797.

Richards MP, Pettitt PB, Trinkaus E, Smith FH, Paunović M, Karavanić I, (2000). Neanderthal diet at Vindija and Neanderthal predation: The evidence from stable isotopes. Proc Natl Acad Sci USA 97 (13): 7663-7666.

Rotman A, (2005). The Roboust Australopithecines: Evidence for the genus Paranthropus. The University of Western Ontario Journal of Anthropology 13(1): 80-84.

Salque M, Bogucki PI, Pyzel J, Sobkowiak-Tabaka I, Grygiel R, Szmyt M, Evershed EP, (2012). Earliest evidence for cheese making in the sixth millennium BC in northern Europe. Nature 493: 522-525.

Shultz S, Nelson E, Dunbar RIM, (2012). Hominin cognitive evolution: identifying patterns and processes in the fossil and archaeological record. Phil Trans R Soc 367(1599): 2130-2140.

Smithsonian Institute. The Holocene: Impact of Human Development. Department of Paleobiology, National Museum of Natural History, Smithsonian Institute [in line]. [Accessed February 19, 2014]. Available online at: http://paleobiology.si.edu/geotime/main/htmlversion/holocene3.html

Sorensen MV, Leonard WR, (2001). Neandertal energetics and foraging efficiency. J Hum Evol 40(6): 483-495.

Spence LA, Lipscomb ER, Cadogan J, Martin B, Wastney ME, Peacock M, Weaver CM, (2005). The effect of soy protein and soy isoflavones on calcium metabolism in postmenopausal women: a randomizedcrossover study. Am J Clin Nutr 81(4): 916-922.

Sponheimer M, Lee-Thorp JA, (1999). Isotopic Evidence for the Diet of an Early Hominid, Australopithecus africanus. Science 283(5400): 368-370 .

Tang BM, Eslick GD, Nowson C, Smith C, Bensoussan A, (2007). Use ofcalcium or calcium in combination with vitamin D supplementation toprevent fractures and bone loss in people aged 50 years and older: a meta-analysis. Lancet 370(9588): 657-666.

The Nobel Prize Foundation. The Nobel Prize in Physiology or Medicine 1931. Nobelprize [in line]. [Accessed February 17, 2014]. Avalable online at: http://www.nobelprize.org/nobel_prizes/medicine/laureates/1931/

The Paleo Diet [in line]. [Accessed March 5, 2014].

Available online at: http://thepaleodiet.com/

Thompson RC, Allam AH, Lombardi GP, Wann LS, Sutherland ML, Sutherland JD, Soliman MA, Frohlich B, Mininberg DT, Monge JM, Vallodolid CM, Cox SL, Abd el-Maksoud G, Badr I, Miyamoto MI, el-Halim Nur el-Din A, Narula J, Finch CE, Thomas GS, (2013). Atherosclerosis across 4000 years of human history: the Horus study of four ancient populations. Lancet 381(9873): 1211-1222.

Tipple BJ, (2013). Capturing climate variability during our ancestors' earliest days. Proc Natl Acad  Sci USA 110 (4): 1144-1145.

Van Arsdale AP, (2013). Homo erectus - A Bigger, Smarter, Faster Hominin Lineage. Nature Education Knowledge 4(1): 2.

Warburg O, (1965). On the Origin of Cancer Cells. Science 123(3191): 309-314.

Warburg O, (1966). The prime cause and prevention of cancer - Part 1 with two prefaces on prevention. Available online at: http://healingtools.tripod.com/primecause1.html/

Warburg O, Posener , Negelein E, (1924). Ueber den Stoffwechsel der Tumoren. Biochemische Zeitschrift 152: 319-344.

Weisdorf JL, (2005). From foraging to farming: Explaning the Neolithic Revolution. Journal of Economics Survey 19(4): 561-586.

Weiss E, Kislev ME, Hartmann A, (2006). Autonomous Cultivation Before Domestication. Science 312(5780): 1608-1610.

Wood B, Constantino P, (2007). Paranthropus boisei: Fifty years of evidence and analysis. American Journal of Physical

Antrhopology 50: 106-132.

Wynn JG, Sponheimer M, Kimbel WH, Alemseged Z, Reed K, Bedaso ZK, Wilson JN, (2013). Diet of Australopithecus afarensis from the Pliocene Hadar Formation, Ethiopia. Proc Natl Acad Sci USA, doi:10.1073/pnas.1222559110.

Zhu XH, Qiao H, Du F, Xiong Q, Liu X, Zhang X, Ugurbil K, Chen W, (2012). Quantitative imaging of energy expenditure in human brain. Neuroimage 60(4): 2107-2117.

**Chapter 6: Conclusions:**

Brown J, (2012). Mankind must go green or die, says Prince Charles. The Independent (London) [in line]. November 2012. [Accessed Febrero 19, 2014]. Available online at: http://www.independent.co.uk/news/uk/home-news/mankind-m ust-go-green-or-die-says-prince-charles-8347524.html

Cassidy ES, West PC, Gerber JS, Foley JA, (2013). Redefining agricultural yields: from tonnes to people nourished per hectare. Environ Res Lett 8: 034015 (8pp).

Ehrlich PR, Ehrlich AH, (2013). Can a collapse of global civilization be avoided? Proc Natl Acad Sci USA 280(1754): 20122845.

Eshela G, Sheponb A, Makovc T, Milo R, (2014). Land, irrigation water, greenhouse gas, and reactive nitrogen burdens of meat, eggs, and dairy production in the United States. Proc Natl Acad Sci USA 111(33): 11996-12001.

Foley JA, Ramankutty N, Brauman KA, Cassidy ES, Gerber JS, Johnston M, Mueller ND, O'Connell C, Ray DK,

West PC, Balzer C, Bennett EM, Carpenter SR, Hill J, Monfreda C, Polasky S, Rockström J, Sheehan J, Siebert S, Tilman D, Zaks DPM, (2011). Solutions for a cultivated planet. Nature 478: 337-342.

Friel S, Dangour AD, Garnett T, Lock K, Chalabi Z, Roberts I, Butler A, Butler CD, Waage J, McMichael AJ, Haines, A, (2009). Public health benefits of strategies to reduce greenhouse-gas emissions: food and agriculture. The Lancet 374(9706): 2016-2025.

Garnett T, (2009). Livestock-related greenhouse gas emissions: impacts and options for policy makers. Environmental Science and Policy 12(4): 491-503.

Grassini P, Eskridge KM, Cassman KG, (2013). Distinguishing between yield advances and yield plateaus in historical crop production trends. Nature Communications 4: 2918.

Hedenus F, Wirsenius S, Johansson DJA, (2014). The importance of reduced meat and dairy consumption for meeting stringent climate change targets. Climatic Change 124: 79-91.

IDC, (2013). Global food security. First Report of Session 2013–14. International Development Committee, House of Commons, UK Parliament. London, United Kingdom.

IUCN, (2012). Ecosystem Restoration. International Union for Conservation of Nature [in line]. November 2012. [Accessed March 12, 2014]. Available online at: http://www.iucn.org/about/union/commissions/cem/cem_work/c em_restoration/

Jha A, (2013). First hamburger made from lab-grown meat to be served at press conference. The Guardian [in line].

August 2013. [Accessed January 18, 2014]. Available online at: http://www.theguardian.com/science/2013/aug/05/first-hambur ger-lab-grown-meat-press-conference

Landi MA, Renison D, (2010). Forestación con Polylepis australis en suelos erosionados de las Sierras Grandes de Córdoba: evaluación del uso de terrazas y vegetación nodriza. Ecol austral 20(1): 47-55.

Lazzarini N, (2013). El reforestador hormiga de las sierras. Diario DíaaDía [in line]. February 2013. [Accessed January 15, 2014]. Available online at: http://www.diaadia.com.ar/cordoba/reforestador-hormiga-sierra s

Lobell DV, Burke MB, Tebaldi C, Mastrandrea MD, Falcon WP, Naylor RL, (2008). Prioritizing Climate Change Adaptation Needs for Food Security in 2030. Science 319(5863): 607-610.

McMichael A, Powles JW, Butler CD, Uauy R, (2007). Food, livestock production, energy, climate change, and health. The Lancet 370 (9594): 1253-1263.

Meadows DH, Meadows DL, Randers J, Behrens III WW, (1972). The Limits to Growth. New York: Universe Books. ISBN 0-87663-165-0.

Motesahrrei S, Rivas J, Kalnay E, (2014). Human and Nature Dynamics (HANDY): Modeling Inequality and Use of Resources in the Collapse or Sustainability of Societies. Paper available online at: http://www.sesync.org/sites/default/files/resources/motesharrei-rivas-kalnay.pdf

Popp A, Lotze-Campen H, Bodirsky B, (2010). Food consumption, diet shifts and associated non-CO2 greenhouse gases from agricultural production. Glob Environ Chang 20(3): 451-462.

Renison D, Cingolani AM, Suarez R, Menoyo E, Coutsiers C, Sobral A, Hensen I, (2005). The Restoration of Degraded Mountain Woodlands: Effects of Seed Provenance and Microsite Characteristics on Polylepis australis Seedling Survival and Growth in Central Argentina. Restorarion Ecology 13(1): 129-137.

Sample I, (2009). World faces 'perfect storm' of problems by 2030, chief scientist to warn. The Guardian [in line]. March 2009. [Accessed February 19, 2014]. Available online at: http://www.theguardian.com/science/2009/mar/18/perfect-stor m-john-beddington-energy-food-climate

Smitha JB, Schneiderb SH, Oppenheimerd M, Yohee GW, Haref W, Mastrandreac MD, Patwardhang A, Burtonh I, Corfee-Morloti J, Magadzaj CHD, Füsself H, Pittockk AB, Rahmanl A, Suarezm A, van Yperselen J, (2009). Assessing dangerous climate change through an update of the Intergovernmental Panel on Climate Change (IPCC) "reasons for concern". Proc Natl Acad Sci USA 106(11): 4133-4137.

Stehfest E, Bouwman L, van Vuuren DP, den Elzen MGJ, Eickhout B, Kabat P, (2009). Climate benefits of changing diet. Climatic Change 95: 83-102.

Stokstad E, (2010). Could Less Meat Mean More Food? Science 327(5967): 810-811.

Thomas CD, Cameron A, Green RE, Bakkenes M, Beaumont LJ, Collingham YC, Erasmus BFN, Siqueira MF, Grainger A, Hannah L, Hughes L, Huntley B, van Jaarsveld AS, Midgley GF, Miles L, Ortega-Huerta MA, Peterson AT, Phillips

OL, Williams SE, (2003). Extinction risk from climate change. Nature 427: 145-148.

Turner GH, (2008). A comparison of The Limits to Growth with 30 years of reality. Global Environmental Change 18(3): 397-411.

Vaughn KJ, Porensky LM, Wilkerson ML, Balachowski J, Peffer E, Riginos C, Young TP,(2010). Restoration Ecology. Nature Education Knowledge 3(10):66.

www.ingramcontent.com/pod-product-compliance
Lightning Source LLC
Chambersburg PA
CBHW030425290526
45786CB00001B/135